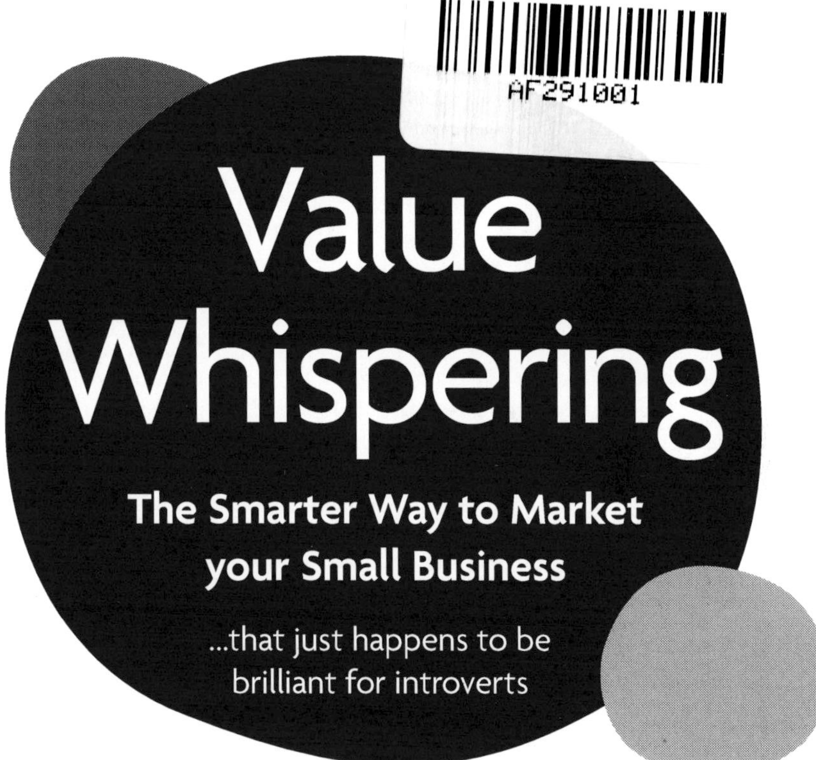

Melitta Campbell

BEST-SELLING AUTHOR OF 'A SHY GIRL'S GUIDE TO NETWORKING'

Value Whispering

First published in Great Britain in 2025 by
Candy Jar Books
136 Newport Rd
Cardiff
CF24 1DJ

Disclaimer: *Value Whispering* is intended for information and education
purposes only. This book does not constitute specific legal, financial
or commercial advice unique to your situation. The author accepts no
responsibility for loss, damage or injury as a direct or indirect result of
reading this book.

Pre-Reader Quotes:

"This book is full of wonderfully simple, and full of practical ideas to help you move forward as a female entrepreneur - thank you Melitta!" **Jennie Reed, Excellence in English**

"This book inspired me to believe I could grow my revenue without sacrificing my authenticity and priorities." **Cath Hodges**

"I was really energized and inspired by this wonderful book. Marketing now feels doable and personable. I feel like I have a way of moving forward that I didn't have before." **Kathy-Ann Edwards, Project Whisperer**

"Melitta has a beautiful knack for making the complex feel simple and the difficult feel doable. The Art of Value Whispering captures her thoughtful, gentle and relatable approach to realise - and finally own - your value with confidence and integrity. All without having to shout louder or burn yourself out. She changes businesses and lives for the better. If you're not going to work with Melitta already – this is the next best thing." **Sapna Pieroux, multi award-winning brand consultant, author and speaker**

"Value whispering sits at the heart of this book, and it shows. Melitta offers a clear, grounded way to market your business without noise or pressure. You see how to share your value, attract your dream clients, and grow in a way that feels aligned. A calm, confident guide for service-based founders. And Melitta is the value whisperer to take you there." **Suman Randhawa, Heart-Led Sales & Messaging Consultant**

"This book is packed with very practical guidance. I particularly loved the message to stop working towards fulfilling your business potential, and instead work from that potential to increase personal and business success." **Nola Heale, The Profit Detective**

"The best thing that Melitta has taught me is that a confused mind doesn't buy. The Value Whispering Blueprint is the perfect method to create clarity, engagement and sales."
Wanda Van Geldren, Mindset and Executive Coach

"What a great book. I only wish I'd been able to read it at the start of my business journey to guide me!" **Jeannie Nairn**

"Finally! A book that gave me a step-by-step seasoned system to build my business successfully—my way, without guilt or comparison. It felt simultaneously like a blanket of encouragement and a nudge in the backside, just when I need it." **Swantje Duncker, Executive Coach**

"I felt surprisingly moved by this book as I felt completely supported throughout. This book shares Melitta's ENTIRE process and is packed with practical tips shared with a clear context and structure. In every section I found myself thinking: "Oh, I could do that!". It's a highly readable, enjoyable and clever book." **Rita Hughes**

"Melitta proves that you don't have to be loud, pushy or everywhere to successfully attract clients. Her approach is perfect for introverts ready to create a real impact with their business."
Matthew Pollard, bestselling author of *The Introvert's Edge* series

"If marketing makes you want to run and hide, read this book. Melitta shows you how to attract dream clients by being more you. No shouting, no cringe, no burnout required."
Andrew and Pete, Founders of Atomicon

Contents

Chapter Eight: Successful Sales Conversations   105

Your sales conversations can be highly valuable experiences that serve your client deeply and help them enjoy better outcomes.

Chapter Nine: Onboarding and Nurturing Your Clients   119

Onboarding isn't just about admin. It's about kickstarting your relationship with your new client, and setting the tone for their success story.

PART THREE
SELF-LEADERSHIP   127

There is a lot we can do to manage our energy, time, focus and mindset. When we set boundaries around what works for us, there is no limit to the positive impact we can create for ourselves and others.

Chapter Ten: Finding the Time and Energy for Growth   129

Focus and productivity are personal. If it works for you, it works.

You don't have to be loud to make a difference, but you do need to be consistently visible to your dream clients. Your mindset is the key to doing so comfortably.

You don't have to be the loudest to be successful. The key is to be aligned with your values, so your every action has purpose and meaning.

The Art of Value Whispering™

Release your diamond within and proudly let your True Value shine.

Two months after the birth of my first daughter, it became clear that returning to the corporate career I loved was not going to be possible. Not wanting to withdraw from my career completely, I started a communication consultancy during nap times, and within a year I was advising communication teams and leaders within some of the world's largest organisations, such as Lloyds Bank, Nestlé and the UN.

It was exciting at first, and I loved the chance to be the kind of Mum I wanted to be, while still getting to use my marketing and communication skills to earn an income. Eight years on I looked like a big success. But on the inside, I found myself facing burnout. I had forgotten to ask myself an all-important question: Why? As a result, I was attracting well-paid contracts, but it wasn't work that gave me joy, meaning and energy. Every day became a chore.

Then I read a quote that changed everything: "If it's no longer fun, stop doing it". Sir Richard Branson's words hit home for me instantly. Heeding his advice, I looked for a different way to use my skills and experiences to help others.

Then something odd started happening.

I'd tell people about my work. How I helped corporate leaders to engage their teams, and communicate complex change projects in a straightforward, human-centric way. I'd talk about the workshops I had designed to help communication professionals think differently about the impact they created and how they approached their work. And after listening to my introduction, without fail, someone would ask me, 'Will you help me build my business?'

I was confused. I was a marketing and communication expert working for corporate leaders, not an expert in small business strategy. And as I couldn't see how I could help, I would always answer 'No'.

That was until I met Ana. She wasn't taking no for an answer. 'But you *have* to help,' she exclaimed. 'You're the only one who can!'

Ana was the sixth person to ask for my help in this way. Faced with her confidence and determination, I realised she saw in me something that I myself had missed.

'You're not the first person to ask me for help building their business,' I said. 'But I'm not sure how I can help. What do you think I have to offer you?'

Ana told me about her business. How she was self-employed and passionate about guiding her coaching clients to results well beyond what they expected. The problem was, she wasn't attracting enough of the right people to create a sustainable business. And even when she *did* get in front of an ideal prospect, they didn't understand her offer in a way that made them want to work with her. At least not without some serious cajoling and discounting.

She was open about how exhausted and disappointed she was feeling. She was a smart woman, and she didn't understand why building a sustainable business was proving such an impossible challenge. She felt as though she was missing a piece of the marketing puzzle, but try as she might, she just couldn't figure out what it was.

'I'm putting more and more time into my business to try and make it work. But then I feel so guilty that I'm not spending time with my family – the very reason I started my business. And when I *am* with my family, I feel guilty that I'm not putting time into my business. The worst part is, I'm starting to feel that my "business" is actually just an expensive hobby. I feel so stuck, like I'll never find a way to feel successful.'

Then she looked me in the eye. 'You help people communicate their ideas in a way that resonates with others, helps them understand and buy into those ideas, and then take the right next step. I get the sense that this is the missing piece I'm searching for. So, will you help me?'

Ana was right. She had described exactly what I did. But I was so close to my work with corporates that I couldn't see how my experience could apply to small business owners.

That night, I replayed our conversation in my mind, and I started to see how I could help Ana and others like her. I realised that she was only partially right. It wasn't her ideas that she needed to communicate; it wasn't her offer; it was the *value* of these. That was the missing piece.

Once she identified this value, and was able to clearly communicate it, not just through her words but through every aspect of the client experience, things would change for her business. She would start to stand out as the obvious choice for her dream clients.

Ana wasn't clear about her value and how to whisper it through her words, her actions and her work, and that was why she was struggling.

Who is ever taught how to communicate professionally? Let alone to communicate the one thing that most makes them brilliant? Who is ever taught how to celebrate what they have to offer, without coming across as pushy or arrogant?

Yet doing so is not just a missing piece of the puzzle – it's the essential corner pieces around which everything else arranges so that the picture comes together.

As I lay awake that night, considering Ana's situation, I realised I'd seen it before. Many of the leaders I worked with shied away from communicating proactively with their teams. They weren't clear how to do it well, and worse, they worried that others would notice their lack of skill and assume they weren't competent in other areas of their work.

Even many of the communication professionals I worked with had never received formal marketing or communication training. There was clearly a big gap, both in terms of skill and confidence, and I had the knowledge, experience and ability to help fill it. I had those missing corner pieces in my hand, and I was excited to share them.

My mind started racing. I imagined what would happen if everyone with a passion for helping others could stop self-eclipsing. What if they no longer allowed their abilities and achievements to be obscured? Or let self-doubt, fear of judgement or negative beliefs limit their potential? I thought about how different the world would be if everyone could use their talents where they were most needed – could share their expertise with those most in need of their unique brand of help. Just imagine if everyone had the support they needed to comfortably communicate their True Value and intentionally live their best lives. Think of the positive ripple effect that could create.

I didn't get much sleep that night. But I didn't care. I was inspired and excited. At 4am I gave up even trying to switch off. Instead, I got up, made a big mug of coffee, fired up my laptop, and started mapping out my thoughts.

If I was going to do this, I knew I needed to cover more than just how to communicate and market a business. Focusing on these alone wouldn't be enough to help people achieve lasting results. Three experiences drove this conviction.

1. During my corporate career, alongside my day job, I had established and led a women's network. This had taught me that having great skills, and believing in your ability to make a difference with those skills, were two different things. For my work to really have an impact, my clients would need to both understand their value *and* believe in it.

2. I knew that many business owners started their business to have greater flexibility. They needed a way to work around their family, studies, or other commitments. Since my clients were likely to be time-poor and have fragmented focus, I'd need to help them find a way to get things done and feel accomplished around their other commitments.

3. Finally, as mentioned earlier, from my work coaching leaders I knew that few people are ever taught how to communicate, let alone how to communicate their own brilliance. I would need to fill this gap by helping my clients quickly grasp the essentials of communication, marketing and sales best practice.

Over the next four weeks, I mapped out the three core elements I wanted to cover: Identifying Your True Value (clarifying your values and vision, and creating the right offers for the right clients), Value Weaving (mastering meaningful marketing and sales), and Self-Leadership (building your CEO mindset, habits and productivity).

Today, I call this process The Value Whispering™ Blueprint. It's illustrated in the diagram below:

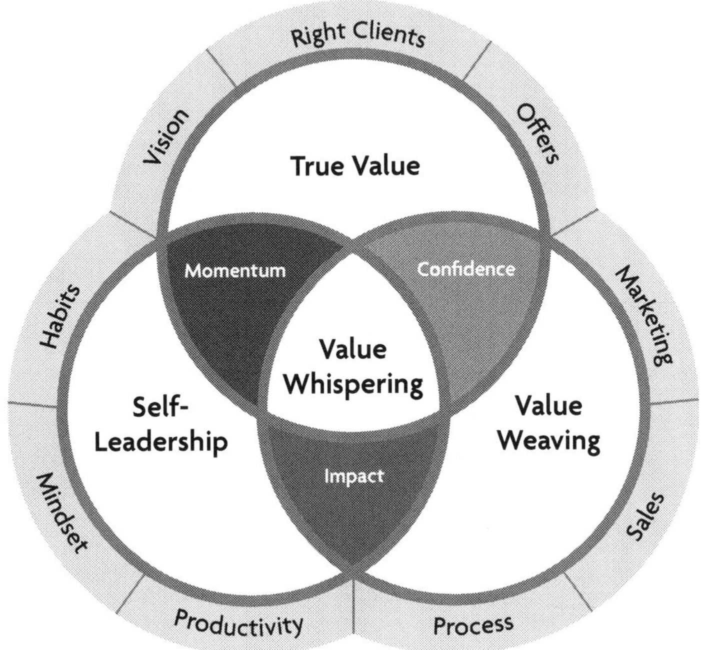

Since I started guiding business owners through this blueprint in 2018, the process has remained largely unchanged. It has helped hundreds of service business owners, like coaches, consultants and course developers, to communicate, market and sell their True Value in a way that feels natural and in alignment with their values and the impact they want to create.

Throughout this book, my goal is to help you understand this blueprint and how you can use it to enjoy the same results, without ever feeling pushy, being fake or becoming overwhelmed. Because, from working with an array of small business owners, I've discovered a few immutable truths.

The Immutable Truths of Marketing Your Own Business

1. Even if you have marketing experience, promoting yourself and your own business feels awkward and often intimidating.

2. While everything is 'figureoutable', researching, trying and testing out what works is draining and always takes longer than you expect.

3. Understanding the right way to market your business is hard. Worse, with all the conflicting advice available, you can quickly feel so overwhelmed and inadequate that you overthink everything and never take the actions required.

4. For most people, trying to attract clients by simply posting more often, or being louder, more outspoken or controversial than the next person doesn't work or feel comfortable.

5. There is never enough time for everything you feel you *should* or *must* be doing. Therefore, it's easy to feel like you are failing or not good enough, even when you're making great progress.

By understanding Value Whispering™, you'll be able to bypass these challenges and pitfalls, and instead create a simple and meaningful message, marketing plan and sales process that you can deliver consistently and with confidence.

The Art of Value Whispering™

Value Whispering™ is the art of intentionally weaving your True Value through everything you do, so that you stand out as the obvious choice for your dream clients. It ensures that no matter how soft your voice, you can resonate deeply with the right people and create a powerful impact.

Value Whispering blends tried and tested 'old-school' marketing techniques with what I've seen work over my three decades in the marketing industry. That thirty-plus years (where did *that* time go?) includes sixteen marketing my own businesses, as well as coaching other business owners – not all introverts, but always people who want to market their business in a way that feels authentic, meaningful and impactful instead of false, loud and pushy.

When these business owners come to me, they're often wondering why their marketing feels so exhausting and ineffective. They're doing all the things they think they *should* be doing, but it's not working.

When marketing feels this way, it's rarely because someone isn't trying hard enough. It's because they're following the wrong approach. They're using strategies that don't fit who they are, the experience they want to create for their clients, or the value they truly offer. Real marketing starts with understanding your clients deeply and then communicating how you can help in a way that feels natural for you *and* meaningful for them.

People with a problem want to understand who can help them solve it and how they will do so. So when you put your customer understanding at the heart of every decision and every action you take, your marketing starts to feel meaningful and even desirable.

In other words, marketing isn't about you; it's about who you help and how. This is great news if you don't relish being the centre of attention.

But a word of warning: you don't want to fall into the trap of doing everything you feel like you 'should' for your clients. Instead, you want to deliver value in a way that feels in complete alignment with their needs and your truth. It's when you show up as your authentic self that you have the most impact. Finding this truth is the starting point of the Value Whispering™ Blueprint and, I believe, the foundation of effective marketing.

This customer-first approach has always felt more natural to me. But it's been a big shift in thinking for many of the people I've trained and coached over the years. This is partly because it's personal: personal to you, your clients and your business goals. It's not about doing the same as anyone else; it's about being different, standing out, and offering a transformation no one else can. That way, you can naturally stand out, make a difference and avoid having to compete on price.

In larger companies, marketing and sales are two different functions. However, most of the business owners I've worked with perform both activities themselves, at least at first. Therefore, I've included a simple sales process within the Value Whispering™ Blueprint. This method continues the value weaving from your marketing, through your sales process and conversations, and into your onboarding and ultimate delivery of your services. It creates a smooth path for your clients to follow, and one you can deliver with confidence.

I've been using Value Whispering™ throughout my business journey, and the recognition I have received proves that it works.

For example, for three years in a row (2021-2023) Acquisition International awarded me Most Influential Female Business Coach (Europe). In 2021, LinkedIn named me as one of the sixteen sales influencers to follow and one of their fifteen most authentic contributors. In 2023, Grant Cardone and Pete Vargas, two of the best-known entrepreneurs in the US, invited me to be a judge at their Great American Speak Off event in Las Vegas, an event that attracted a live audience of 40,000, with thousands more following the event online. In 2024, I was invited to give a TEDx talk about Value Whispering, and my thought leadership has been featured in many publications, including *Thrive Global*, *Fast Company* and *Forbes*.

I don't share this to brag, but to show you that you don't need to be loud or outspoken to get noticed, be remembered and to create impact. When you have a business that sets out to make a positive difference in the world, you can design your marketing to do the same.

And that positive difference isn't just external. When your marketing creates intentional value, your confidence, pride and self-belief also grows. And with it, your ability to dream bigger and achieve more than you initially thought possible.

That's what I find so exciting. When I start working with a new client, I can never quite be sure what they will create by the end of our time together. But it's always something better, brighter or bigger than either of us could have imagined in our first meeting.

In this book, I will take you through each of the elements of the Value Whispering™ Blueprint so you too can start to believe in your value and communicate it clearly and confidently. By following the steps, you will build a solid personal brand, show up consistently, and create a business that you feel proud of.

When I think about the Value Whispering™ process, an image springs to mind: following the blueprint feels like mining for that diamond within.

First, you have to dig deep to find that seam, rich in potential value.

Then you chip away at the rock to reveal the precious stone.

Then you give it a shape suitable for its final purpose.

Then, finally, you polish and proudly share it with the world.

And when you do, the light hits your diamond and refracts in all directions, casting dozens of small beams that cast rainbows on any surface they touch. Some small, some large, but all beautiful.

When you whisper your value through everything you do, you create this wonderful kaleidoscope effect that creates positive impacts in all sorts of unexpected ways.

I can't wait to see what happens when you share your diamond with the world.

But before we embark on this journey, I want you to keep the following Dos and Don'ts in mind:

Our Rules of Engagement

1.   DO: Trust yourself and the process.

It might not feel like it now, but you already have everything you need to follow and complete this process. I promise.

My goal isn't to overload you with new information and activities you must do to get clients. Instead, the purpose of this book is to bring to the surface everything that is already amazing about you and your service. Once we have identified your True Value, we can start weaving this through everything you do to create an impactful brand and meaningful marketing strategy without having to be someone you're not.

2.   DO: Be kind to yourself.

Any process of evolution is a challenge. As you follow this book, you will likely experience moments when you feel overwhelmed or not ready. This is normal. It often indicates that you are at the tipping point between having the information you need, and knowing what to do with it.

In these moments, take a break. Do something you love, something that nourishes your soul. Remind yourself that you are brilliant, and that you can get through this, just like you've gotten through so many other hard times in the past. Then, when you feel ready, keep going.

3.   DO: Be bold.

You can only discover your True Value if you are honest about your skills and strengths. Typically, we underplay these. As you follow this book, I want you to do the opposite. Be bold. You have my full permission to brag – after all, no one else needs to see the work you do here.

Embrace your skills and talents. Internalise the praise you've received over the years. And allow yourself to feel proud of what makes you different and amazing.

4. DON'T: Wait to get things perfect.

By the end of this book, your messaging, marketing and sales will be better than they are today. But that doesn't mean you should wait to make connections, build your community, post on social media or have conversations about your business.

What you can do today is already more than good enough to have an impact. Start where you are. Don't worry about being perfect; focus on being yourself and bring your audience along for the journey.

5. DON'T: Compare yourself, your speed or your success to anyone else's journey.

Embrace and celebrate your difference, knowing that it is exactly what your dream clients want. They don't want a carbon copy of someone else; they want and appreciate *you*.

Be inspired by other people's ideas and achievements, but never allow their apparent success to diminish your belief in your own ability to create an impact.

6. DON'T: Ever use the words 'should' or 'must'.

Let go of any pressure or expectations to do or perform a certain way, or to get things perfect. Instead, embrace your own instincts, follow your curiosity and listen to your inner knowing, even if the outcome of that path isn't yet clear.

Remember, if it works for you, it works.

7. DON'T: Go through this alone.

Over the last five years, I've interviewed more than 200 successful business owners on my podcast. One of the most consistent pieces of advice they share is: don't build your business alone.

Build a team of advisors or invest in a coach. And surround yourself with people who inspire you, believe in your vision, and can support and encourage you along the way. This needn't be expensive. Find people through in-person or online networks, or come and join the Value Whispering Circle. It's my online community, and it's full of incredible coaches, consultants and service-based business owners, all ready to support and encourage you. Within that community, I also share regular live masterclasses on Value Whispering™ to help you put into practice everything you learn here. And it's completely free. You'll find more details at: www.melittacampbell.com/club

There is one last rule I have for you before we get started. When I speak with business owners like Ana, they often have a nagging feeling they're missing something. They want to work smart. They want to be able to prioritise their work so they can balance marketing their business with serving their clients. And they want to feel like everything they are doing is right and worthwhile.

They are looking for that magic something that will tie all their marketing together and make it all work. They are looking to understand and to share their True Value. *This* is the first step in any business; *this* is the piece of the puzzle that remains missing for many. It's what compelled me to write this book, and why I'm so happy that you took the initiative to not only select this title, but to read it.

But don't stop there. Reading this book alone won't make any difference to your business. Only taking action will. Remember that. Any time you find yourself nodding along, stop. Take a note of what resonated with you, and think about what you will do with that information. How will you use that insight to move your business forward?

So, the final rule is:

8.   DO: Make notes, highlight your insights, and take action.

Yes, with this rule I'm giving all you good girls and boys full permission to write on the pages of this book! However, if you simply can't bring yourself to, I've created some insight-to-action sheets you can download, along with other resources to support you as you create your Value Whispering™ Blueprint, from: www.melittacampbell.com/ValueWhisperingBook

In the next chapter, I'll show you how to start revealing your True Value. This is an exciting, empowering and joyful process. You'll start to see yourself, and what's possible for you, in a whole new light!

Stepping into your brilliance often goes against what we've been taught or how we've been conditioned. It can feel scary, even wrong.

If these feelings come up for you as you work through the chapter, I want you to know that this is normal, and I'm here by your side every step of the way.

You can do this.

You are brilliant.

Your work matters.

Your voice is powerful.

Let's prove it!

Part One

Understanding Your True Value

*Once you know your True Value, you'll
start to naturally stand out as the
obvious choice for your Dream Clients,
and they'll start to come to you.*

Most business owners who struggle with marketing aren't struggling with the *act* of marketing. They're struggling because, on the surface, it feels shallow. It feels as though they are just 'doing stuff' to be seen rather than contributing something meaningful to the world. They know they need to market their business, but without a deeper connection, the whole process can feel fluffy, forced or even pointless.

And for the most part, they're right.

If you jump into marketing too soon (which I see all the time) you skip the most important step — the step that connects *you* to your marketing, and that creates something so relevant and valuable to your Dream Clients that they feel drawn to you. When you get this part right, everything else becomes clearer, easier and more meaningful.

It starts with understanding your unique combination of lived experiences, natural talents, learned skills, values and perspectives. Then it continues by considering how you can use these qualities to solve your clients' problems in a way only *you* can. This is your True Value.

When you know this value, and own it, you stop competing in a noisy marketplace and start naturally standing out as the obvious choice for the right people, in the right way, at the right time.

In this part of the book, we'll uncover what makes you *you*, identify your Dream Clients, and explore how your unique mix of strengths and experiences make you their ideal service provider. By the end of Part One, you'll have a clear picture of the value you bring, the people you're here to serve, and how to connect the two so your work feels not only successful, but deeply fulfilling and meaningful.

Chapter One

Your True Value

No matter how soft your voice, you can create a powerful impact.

I developed my Value Whispering™ approach over years of working as a marketer for small businesses, large businesses and non-profits, and more recently as a coach for solopreneurs and coaches.

But there was one experience that kick-started it all.

I started my career working for two medium-sized companies. I had a range of responsibilities – marketing, client-communications and brand – and within those roles, I was also responsible for PR, an aspect of my work that I really enjoyed.

So, when I was offered a job focusing solely on PR, I jumped at the chance. The fact that it came with a significant leap in salary was a nice bonus. For the first time, I was working as part of a marketing and PR team, and I enjoyed having colleagues to bounce ideas off and learn from.

Everything was going perfectly, so when the CEO unexpectedly asked me to come to work on a Sunday for a special board meeting, I was excited. On the train from London to St Albans, my mind started to race with all the possible reasons for the meeting. Perhaps we were going to launch a new supercomputer that would revolutionise the future of learning? Maybe we were going to take over another company?

But as the meeting began, I soon realised that this wasn't about the future of the company, but its end. The company was going into receivership with immediate effect!

'Does this mean I've lost my job?!' I asked.

The CEO turned to me, and in his eyes, I could see the dawning realisation that he perhaps should have briefed me before the meeting. 'Yes,' he replied slowly, 'I'm so sorry.'

So, there it was. My dream job was ending, just six weeks after it had begun. I felt crushed.

Over the next six months, I applied for countless jobs and failed at dozens of interviews. I was starting to lose hope that I'd ever find a new position, and my savings were almost spent.

Then I applied for a job within the British government's communication pool. My application was accepted, and I was invited to submit a communications strategy for a scenario they provided. They liked my strategy, and I was invited to a full day of tests and an interview.

On the train into London, I felt nervous but excited. As I happily clutched the train ticket I'd bought with my last £5, I had no idea that this day would become one of the worst and most humiliating experiences of my life.

The day started with a group exercise. Then we had to write an article and complete two tests. The last part of the day was a panel interview. Walking in for this final stage, I felt confident and optimistic. But ten minutes later, the lead interviewer threw my CV back in my face, shouting at me to 'GET OUT!'

'Is this part of the interview?' I asked, in shock.

'No, it is not. Get out of my sight. I can't listen to any more of your lies!'

'I don't understand. I haven't been lying. Why would you say that?'
Then she dropped the bombshell...

"I've been sitting here listening to you. And all you've said is: '*We* did this...' and '*We* did that...' I can only conclude that you are passing off someone else's work as your own, and I won't have anyone in my team who steals credit from other people. Now get out!'

I tried to explain that I'd spent the last seven years working for small companies, and I had been the sole person developing marketing and PR strategies *and* doing the work. But it was too late.

I left the room desperately trying to hold back the tears. But once out of the building, there was no stopping them. It felt like the end of the world!

But three days later, when my pity-fog finally cleared, the penny dropped. She was right! Not that I'd stolen credit from anyone else – but I'd willingly given away mine.

Growing up, I was a shy child. I always felt so nervous in social situations. Family gatherings, neighbours' Christmas parties, even entering the school yard each morning filled me with dread.

When adults asked me questions, I tended to murmur my answers. This prompted them to speak over me, causing me to feel embarrassed and insignificant. So, at a very early age, I concluded that my ideas and stories were not interesting or valuable to anyone else, and I should keep them to myself.

This strategy served me well – for a while, at least. I became the classic 'good girl'. I kept my head down, worked hard and was a great team player. And this continued into adulthood. I always referred to my wins as team or company successes. But now, in the aftermath of my disastrous interview, I could see that my 'quiet and safe' strategy was holding me back. *We* really hadn't achieved these wins – *I* had achieved them.

This moment woke me up to my need to change. Many people never receive this wake-up-call, or when they do, they miss it. They fail to see their True Value and therefore fail to intentionally express it. Then, sooner or later, they experience that nagging sense that they were meant for more and ask: 'Is this it?'

Honestly, who is ever encouraged to talk about their brilliance? I certainly wasn't. Most of us learn, one way or another, that talking about our strengths and successes is bragging or being full of yourself, and that's bad. On the other hand, we are also taught that talking about our failures and struggles shows weakness, and that's also bad.

That leaves us in the middle, feeling the same, saying the same, and doing the same as everyone else. And that is not a space from which we can stand out and make a difference. That's a space where we blend in and become invisible. Or get thrown out of interviews, accused of lying.

So, the first step in Value Whispering™ is to courageously explore your True Value: all your natural talents, learned wisdom and core values. Everything you've learned from books, life, your triumphs and your mistakes. Get it all out there and embrace it. Appreciate how every misstep, every encounter – good or bad – has shaped the person you are today. You'll gain a fresh perspective on everything that makes you *you*.

Here are some steps you can take to help you.

Understand Your Values

Download a list of values. I have put one together for you in the resources that accompany this book at: www.melittacampbell.com/ ValueWhisperingBook

Read through the list and circle all those values that resonate with you. Then go back through your shortlist and choose the three that are most important to you. If you struggle with this, compare values by choosing two and asking yourself: 'If I could have x but not y, would that concern me?'

Now you have your final three, take some time to reflect on what they mean. How do they show up in your work and your interactions with others? How do you know when you are acting in alignment with these values? How do you feel when you are not? As much as possible, try and visualise or express how these values guide you. This will build your awareness and help you to live these values more often. Write down your three values and put this somewhere visible as a daily reminder of who you want to be.

(Side note: if certain values don't make it into your final three, this doesn't mean they aren't important to you; they are just not the *most* important. For example, if you didn't choose 'honesty' as a value, it doesn't follow that you are dishonest.)

Explore Your Strengths

Sometimes our strengths can feel so natural to us that they are more obvious to others than to ourselves. I mentioned earlier that many of us learn to keep our talents hidden for fear of being seen as full of ourselves (as if we could ever be full of anything else). That can make the following exercise challenging. A few years ago, when I was running a personal branding workshop, I asked participants to list their strengths and weaknesses. At the end of the exercise, most people had a list of weaknesses running off the page but had only listed two or three strengths. Not only that, but some of the weaknesses were irrelevant. One person wrote 'I'm hopeless at playing guitar', and when I asked why that was important, they told me that it wasn't, and they didn't even want to play!

Some of their weaknesses were skills gaps. If you are, for example 'no good at presenting', this is something you can improve with learning and practice. If such skills are important to you or achieving your goals, move them onto a separate 'skills I'd like to improve' list, then determine what actions you can take to start turning them into strengths.

By strengths, I don't mean individual tasks or functions, I mean the traits that we express through our work. Some of us are punctual; some of us empathetic; some of us show great initiative and can take an idea and run with it without further guidance or supervision. It doesn't particularly matter what specific responsibilities we are tasked with – these traits will shine through regardless. *That* is what I mean by a strength.

While you are thinking things over, remember that some so-called weaknesses can also be considered strengths – like the classic: perfectionism. If your perfectionism causes you to overthink, procrastinate and hold yourself back, it can be a flaw. But it also highlights that you pay attention to detail, hold yourself to high standards, and have a desire to make an important difference. So, check your weaknesses for hidden strengths that, instead of suppressing, you can lean into.

Because finding your strengths can be challenging, it's good to get outside help. You can visit www.viacharacter.org to take a free online strengths assessment. And/or you can ask some of your most trusted friends and colleagues this question: 'What have you noticed that I do well, perhaps better than most, that I might not have noticed myself?' Be prepared to do the same for them if they ask you in return. Try to get at least five answers so you can see the patterns across their responses. Then reflect on what this tells you about your strengths and values.

Skills and Talents

This is a fun one to explore. Create three columns on a page. On the first column, list five (or more) jobs you had in the past. Then in the middle column, for each job, list the activities you most enjoyed doing and your most notable successes. Then in the final column, note down what this tells you about you and your ability to make success happen. Once you've finished this exercise, put it aside for at least twenty-four hours, then review your lists and reflect on what they tell you about the many ways in which you are brilliant.

Leverage Your Hard-Won Insights

At school, we're often taught that failure is bad. Failure results in bad grades, and bad grades condemn us to a career cleaning toilets (or at least that's what Mr Jenkins told me and my Year Four classmates). With such dire lessons learned, we come to fear failure and dare not admit when we've messed up. This lesson is further drummed into us when we start work. We soon learn that, if we fail to meet our targets, our annual bonus – even our job itself – might be at risk.

But there are few things we get right first time, especially when trying new things and pushing our boundaries. No one gets far in business by playing it safe. And no *you* has ever before built *your* business. Mistakes and failures are inevitable as you figure things out, and these mistakes are an important part of the process. They will teach you everything you need to know about what it takes for you to succeed.

We should therefore celebrate our failures with the same rigour and joy as we do our successes. Those hard-won insights are highly valuable, both to ourselves and others. They add practical experience to our natural talents, learned expertise and personal values.

List all your mistakes and rumble with what each one taught you. Consider what these experiences added to your value, and how these lessons can be incorporated into your work to help you stand out and generate meaning for yourself and others.

Now you've reflected on what is important to you, on your strengths, what you do well, and how you might improve. You've explored all aspects of you and your learned and lived experiences, and the connections between them. This is your True Value; embrace it. You'll soon see that you've been gifted a one-of-a-kind perspective.

Take my client Catherine. At first, she struggled to figure out her unique True Value. As a health coach, she had read the same research as her peers and achieved many of the same certifications. At first look, even her values seemed similar. Then she told me her story, and everything came together.

She told me about how, aged forty, she'd looked at herself in the mirror and hadn't liked what she'd seen. She looked old and constantly felt tired. She found herself snapping at her kids and felt disappointed that she wasn't the fun and energetic mum she wanted to be. But she also thought this was normal for a busy woman of her age.

By the time of our first meeting, aged fifty-two, Catherine was in the best shape of her life. She told me how she believed that women were being told a lie about their health, and how it's not all downhill after forty. This realisation made her determined to help women understand that they can improve their health at any age, and to help them find their own, realistic path to better health and energy.

This wasn't something that every health coach goes through. This was unique to Catherine. When she realised this, she started speaking about her work differently. From her very next social media post, she was changing lives for the better. Without her having to work harder or be louder, clients and opportunities started to show up. As her True Value became easy to see, she naturally stood out to the right people.

Embracing Your True Value

Now you have deeper insight into every aspect of your value, it's time to decide how to use it. While all insight is worthwhile, it might not all be relevant right now. Use the following questions to help take your value and put it into context.

1. What do you most love/hate to see happen for your Dream Clients?

2. How does your True Value help them to enjoy different results?

3. Why will your Dream Clients appreciate you and your approach? What will they love most?

4. How do you want to show up as your client's champion?

Review your answers and reduce this sentiment down to three words that remind you of how you want to be, so you can show up with consistency and intention.

Remember the interview I was thrown out of in my twenties? Well, two weeks later, in my very next interview, I experienced the power of Value Whispering™ for the very first time.

In this interview, I talked about and owned my achievements. I openly shared my failures and the lessons they taught me. I proudly stated my values, perspectives and my vision for the future. And guess what? Before I'd even reached my front door, they called to say I had got the job!

On my first day, my new boss told me that they had been 'blown away' by my interview.

By embracing every aspect of my value, and clearly showing how I could use my unique qualities to make a difference, my results changed. In whispering my value, I had become the obvious choice.

Now I'd discovered what it really took for me to succeed, I continued to whisper my value through everything I did. And as I did so, I started to stand out; in turn, I received regular promotions and was invited to join interesting projects that supported both my personal and career growth.

And I've seen my business clients have the same success when they follow my Value Whispering™ Blueprint. Often within weeks, they come to be seen as the obvious choice for their Dream Clients, and they begin to feel a new pride in their impact on their markets. This includes those with a quieter personality, reinforcing my belief that success doesn't come from being louder, but from resonating deeper.

You've taken the first step to becoming aware of your True Value. Now it's time to see how you can use it to make a positive difference in the world. This starts with identifying your Dream Clients, and considering how your value can help them enjoy better outcomes in life.

CHAPTER SUMMARY

- Own your achievements and value. Recognising and owning your achievements is essential to being seen and understood for your true worth.

- Courageously explore your True Value. Your value is made up of your natural talents, learned skills, core values, lived experiences, and the lessons you learned from both successes and failures. Actively identify and embrace all these elements.

- Shift the narrative from blending in to standing out. Cultural conditioning often teaches us not to talk about our strengths or struggles, leaving us doing and saying the same as everyone else. In other words, we make ourselves invisible. By confidently communicating your values, strengths and unique perspective, you naturally stand out and resonate more deeply with your dream clients.

- Success comes from resonating deeper, not being louder. The key to attracting the right clients and opportunities is in showing how your True Value creates better outcomes for others. When you whisper your value clearly and authentically through everything you do, you naturally stand out as the obvious choice for your dream clients.

Chapter Two

Your Dream Clients

*Only working with your Dream Clients
will grow your business.*

Hopefully you are beginning to see yourself and your value in a new light. It's now time to turn your attention to your clients. Who do you want to work with and how would you like to impact their lives?

At this point, it's tempting to proudly announce that everyone in your market is a potential client, or to only slightly narrow that broad niche of potential customers, excluding the worst of the worst, but keeping the vast majority in your sights.

But to start this chapter, I want to help you to understand that only your Dream Clients will grow your business. And by Dream Clients, I don't mean "everyone", and neither I do mean "almost everyone".

I know this concept can be challenging. You have a big heart and a genuine desire to help as many people as you can; focusing on just one clear client group can feel daunting. But I believe it is the single most important thing you can do to support your business's success. Not to mention your own sanity! You can target more client groups as your business grows and evolves, but to start with, focus on one group only.

Not everyone will be your Dream Client, and that's perfectly okay. It's crucial to work with clients who align with your values, respect your processes, and are genuinely committed to getting results. These clients will appreciate your expertise, boost your confidence, save you time, energy and resources, and refer you to other people just like them, contributing to the growth of your business.

By contrast, working with the wrong clients can destroy your business, and fast. You may feel that, to get started, anyone willing to pay you is worthwhile. But working with the wrong clients can be a slippery slope. This was exactly what led me to burn out while working on my first business. While I was attracting high-paying clients, and doing work I could do well, it wasn't work that felt fulfilling and energising. I could keep going for a while, but I soon started to feel the effects on my energy and mental health.

The clients flying the biggest red flags were those who didn't value my work. These clients fell into three camps, and it was only through experience that I learned to identify them. The first group, the Rushers, would demand a quick turnaround. This meant I couldn't do my best work, though I would still exhaust myself trying.

The second group, the Discount Seekers, wanted reduced rates or special conditions. Wanting to help, I'd take them on, but since I found it hard to do my best work within the budgeted time, I'd feel guilty and either resent the quality of the work I produced, or work extra (unpaid) time to create work I felt proud of.

The third group, the Boundary Breakers, would often start well, but then keep demanding more than was originally agreed and/ or constantly question everything. Their negativity left me feeling drained, and because I'd have to do work that fell outside of my zone of genius, their constant nitpicking made me doubt my abilities and exhaust myself to please them.

If you take on too many red flag clients, before you can say "breakeven", you've either given up, burnt out or gone bankrupt. This may seem extreme, but I've experienced it myself, not to mention seen it happen to countless others. Be aware of who your red flag clients are and how they show up. Often this awareness comes from experience, but as a starting point, you can borrow my hard-won lessons. Avoid Rushers, Discount Seekers and Boundary Breakers in your business: anyone who exhibits this kind of behaviour – who pushes for unrealistic deadlines, who tries to squeeze you for every last penny, who demands more and more and disregards what was agreed – is a red flag client, and they're not worth your time and energy.

Knowing who your Dream Clients are – what they value, how they behave, and how they discover your business – will help you avoid red flag clients. Refining your messaging and marketing to exclusively target these Dream Clients saves you a lot of time and energy over the long-term. To illustrate this point, let's play a game I call 'Generalist or Specialist'. For each of the following scenarios, I want you to imagine which service provider you would contact first. Ready?

Scenario One: You have just moved from your home in Brazil to Switzerland.

You love your new country. It's so beautiful. But you didn't expect the culture shock to be quite so strong. In Brazil, you were used to a more communal way of life; neighbours dropped in for a coffee unannounced, and feelings were expressed openly, the better for everyone to understand each other and get along. You're not sure how you can stay true to your open and expressive nature *and* fit in with your new quiet, conservative neighbours. You are starting to feel lost and lonely, and you've decided to look for someone who can help you.

Who would you contact first?
A: Sandra: a life coach
B: Pauline: a life coach for women
C: Caroline: a life coach for expat women in Switzerland

Scenario Two: You've been coaching for a couple of years, and you've decided now is the time to get more visible, but you lack confidence. You've identified LinkedIn as the best place for you to be present, as you feel this is where your ideal clients hang out. But being someone who is typically shy and private, you're not sure where to start on the platform. You've decided to invest in some help.

Who would you contact first?
A: Andrew: a social media strategist
B: Kenny: a LinkedIn strategist
C: Jason: the *shh*-trategist, a LinkedIn strategist for introverted coaches

Scenario Three: You're a mum of three school-aged children. You want to learn to ski so you can keep up with your kids on your next ski holiday. But as you are forty-three and starting from scratch, you feel nervous, especially knowing that if you fall, it could really hurt! You've decided to take some lessons.

Who would you contact first?
A: Valerie: a ski instructor
B: Gemma: an English-speaking ski instructor
C: Claire: an English-speaking ski instructor who helps adult learners to ski with confidence so they can keep up with their kids

Hopefully you can now see how, once you know exactly who your Dream Clients are, it becomes easy to position yourself as their obvious first choice.

Perception is everything. When you are seen not only as a specialist, but *the* specialist, your Dream Clients will assume you know exactly how to guide them to the results they seek. They also assume that you are worth the investment. And that means you can charge a premium price for your service – and for most small businesses, only premium pricing enables the level of service that will deliver for both the business and the client.

In other words, when you have a clear niche, the right people will naturally gravitate to you and be happy to pay for your services, whatever your fees. You can avoid any hard-selling and instead focus on hard-serving. You only need to be visible in the right places and consistent in your message. When it comes to your offers, marketing and sales, having a clear niche will do a lot of the hard work for you.

Facing Your Niching Fears

I'm sure that by now you're nodding along and beginning to see the power of narrowing down your niche. But I also know how stubborn our fears can be, particularly if they've been with us for a while. So let me address the most common fears business owners have around this process of identifying and targeting Dream Clients.

1. Fear of Exclusion

A common concern when choosing a niche is that you'll exclude potential clients – meaning they'll miss out on your services, and you'll miss out on potential income. In my experience, however, the opposite is true. As our exercises showed, if you try to appeal to a broad market, you actually attract *fewer* clients. Your value becomes vague, and who wants the generic option when there's another tailored just to them? Not only this, but in your efforts to satisfy everyone, your time and energy are spread too thin, and the standard of your services drops.

Focusing on a clear niche sharpens your offer and helps you communicate its value and outcomes more clearly. And here's the surprising part: this clarity often attracts people *outside* your niche without you even trying.

I see this all the time on my twice-weekly client calls. As soon as someone defines the offer they can deliver most powerfully to their Dream Client, the value of that offer becomes obvious to others in their network. It's not unusual for them to be approached by people outside their niche who say, 'This is exactly the result I'm looking for! Could we work together?'

But at that point, beware of red flags! You get to choose whether they're someone you'd enjoy serving. A diplomatic 'No', maybe even a referral to another business, can save you time, energy and money, in the long run.

2. Fear of Missing Out

It's natural to fear missing out on potential impact and income, especially in the early days of your business. You may be tempted to say 'Yes!' to every opportunity that comes your way, just like I did in my first business. However, trying to say 'Yes' to everything in reality means saying 'No' to opportunities that align better with your True Value and goals.

As we've explored, working with the wrong clients drains your mental capacity and resources. It also prevents you from being able to show up for your Dream Clients and make the positive impact you set out to create.

Since most small businesses have limited time and resources, it makes sense to focus these resources on serving clients you can have the biggest impact for, who you will enjoy serving, and who will happily pay in full for that service.

Your focus will help you become known for your results, and this in turn will attract more of the right people and opportunities to your business. You'll start to feel proud of the impact you create and grow both professionally and financially. It's a virtuous cycle.

3.   Fear of Being Boxed In

Perhaps you fear becoming known for just one thing and getting stuck in the same box forever. If so, I want to assure you that this is rarely the case. As you evolve and gain more experience, it's perfectly acceptable to refine, expand or change your niche to realign with your True Value and growing team or resources.

Where you start in business is never where you end up. I hear evidence of this every week on my podcast, *the Art of Value Whispering* (previously *the Driven Female Entrepreneur*, pre-episode 190). You can start where you are today and then adapt as you go. Embrace the flexibility that comes with being the boss of your own business and allow your niche to evolve as you do.

There are lots of famous examples of this. If you close your eyes and think of Marlboro cigarettes what do you see? If you're like most people, you see a rugged cowboy on a horse. But did you know that Marlboro was originally a well-known brand for women?

Likewise, Nokia became synonymous with mobile telephones, but it was originally a paper company. Avon started out selling books, not beauty products. Starbucks started out selling coffee machines, not serving the final cup. And Wrigley started out making and selling soap – imagine chewing on that!

4.   Fear of Choosing the Wrong Niche

This same advice applies if you are worried about choosing the wrong niche. Don't let that fear stop you from getting started. There is no wrong niche. You can start somewhere that feels feasible right now, and then learn, adapt and grow from there.

If, in time, you decide that you have chosen a niche that you don't want to work with forever, you haven't failed. You've gained valuable information that will allow you to find your Dream Clients and pivot your business to attract and serve them. I'm a firm believer that we often learn more from our mistakes than we do our successes. Getting things wrong can sometimes make your business stronger in the long-term.

However real they feel, many of the fears business owners have around niching are unfounded. Hopefully by now you've been able to put your fears to one side and feel ready to move on to the next chapter, when you will start to find your Dream Clients.

But before we do, I want to introduce you to Monica. When I first met Monica, she had no shortage of clients for her online American English lessons. But too many of those clients were red flags. They weren't paying her full fees on time, failed to turn up regularly and didn't do the work needed between sessions. Monica felt disappointed by their lack of progress and was exhausted trying to help them.

However, once she took a step back and defined her Dream Clients, she found she had a real passion for helping immigrants to thrive at work and within their new community. Within this group, there were three sub-groups, each with a distinct need that she could serve well. Understanding these, Monica was able to create the perfect offer for each group and price them fairly – meaning the price was both accessible to her client and reflected the value she offered, giving her good profit margins.

Within six months, Monica had doubled her profit, was working with clients that she loved to show up for, felt more confident and in control, and she had more time and energy for her partner and hobbies.

When you have a single clear niche, it's far easier to grow your business and have a meaningful impact. Especially if you are an introvert who needs to protect their energy. Engaging with others can be particularly draining for us introverts, and engaging with the wrong people can be exhausting.

Once you are clear about your Dream Client, you can create everything with them in mind. As Monica experienced, this allows you to have more impact, to become known for your results, to enjoy better profits (so you can continue to serve your clients meaningfully over the long term), and to feel confident, in control and energised.

When you understand your niche well and create offers that specifically address your Dream Clients' needs, you will move from reviews like 'It was good', to ones that say 'Wow, that was transformational'. Your clients will give you stronger testimonials and refer you to more people like them, growing your business, while also reducing your marketing effort and costs.

And when your clients consistently confirm the value of your work, your confidence, self-belief, and ability to dream big will blossom.

Over the years, I've had several clients proudly show me their forty-three-slide pitch decks that business strategists created for them. Each one was well designed and had lots of bullet points and numbers, even the odd graph. But none of my clients had implemented anything from these impressive plans. Why? Because there was no detail about the client beyond a few demographic details. There was no 'how'.

So when the plan said:

- Post twice a week to LinkedIn

- Send brochure to key decision makers

- Blah, blah, blah

My clients felt stuck. *What* do I say on LinkedIn? Where do I start with designing my brochure? *How* do I find out who the key decision makers are and *how* do I approach them?

But once you get to know your Dream Client, you'll be able to create content, offers, products and experiences that are specific to their needs and preferences, and ensure you naturally stand out as their ideal choice.

Niching goes beyond demographics. Saying you help women aged forty-plus to find their purpose is a good start. But thinking about people in terms of the categories they fall into is impersonal, and your marketing and communications should be the opposite of that. Who are the people, the real people, that fall into these categories? Who is looking for that kind of support? What difference will it make in their lives? What are they experiencing and feeling today that makes them think they need your service?

The simplest and most effective way is not to market to a 'niche', but to one person. Your marketing and messaging will be clearer, more compelling and more personal for your prospect (not to mention easier for you to create). And you'll start to resonate so deeply that, when your Dream Clients experience you, they won't be able to imagine working with anyone else.

I had a client who described this as 'Side Door Marketing'. She felt that, while everyone else was politely knocking on the front door and introducing themselves, she was able to go through the side door and shout 'Cooee, shall I put the kettle on?' (For those of you who live outside of the UK, the side door of the house typically opens into the garden and is often left unlocked. Friends and family, therefore, use this door to enter the house without knocking.) I love this 'Side Door Marketing' idea. It perfectly expresses the results of Value Whispering™ and marketing to your single Dream Client: even before someone becomes a paying client, you are already a known and valuable part of their world.

So, where do you begin?

Defining Your Dream Client

Depending on your experience in business, the process of defining your Dream Client may be completely new, or it may be a matter of refining or refreshing previous work. Either way, the process is the same.

Answer the following questions, going one level at a time. Then reflect on your answers and what they tell you before moving on to the next level. I recommend that you leave some time between writing your answers and reviewing them, to give your thoughts space and to help you be more objective and able to spot any gaps in your initial thinking.

The questions assume that you have already worked with some clients. If this isn't the case, use your best estimates for now. You will still gain clarity. Once you have worked with some clients, you can come back, test your assumptions against the reality and refine your niche. It's good practice to do this periodically. Remember, where you start is never where you end up. Refining regularly will help you adjust as you go. And 'regularly' is whatever makes sense for you, as it will depend on the speed of your personal and business growth.

Level One: Narrowing your focus

- Who do you love working with and supporting?

- Who values your expertise and the experience you create?

- Who gets the best results from working with you?

- Who can afford to pay you?

- Who can you realistically reach?

For each question, free write until you have exhausted all your thoughts and ideas.

Then go back through your list and underline any of your points that stand out to you. If you've lived on this planet for a while, you have probably written a lot under each point. But that doesn't mean you have to move forward with all of them. Be discerning. Pay attention to how you feel in your body when you read each point. Highlight only those points that resonate with you and spark joy or excitement. And avoid the temptation to underline any points that you feel *should* be on your list. You don't want to build a business that fulfils anyone else's dreams or expectations.

Once you have identified your Dream Client, it's time to dig in deeper and find out who they are.

Level Two: Getting to Know Your Single Dream Client
Use this process to capture what you already know about your Dream Client. You may have already worked with them, or perhaps you yourself were your ideal client a few months or years ago. As before, free write your answers before reviewing and refining them.

- What are their values?

- How do they see themselves?

- What does a typical day look like for them?

- What jobs[1] are they juggling, and why are these important to them?

- What do they wish were different, better or easier?

- What are their aspirations?

---

1   (When I use the word 'Jobs', I don't mean the day job they get paid for, but all the things they are trying to achieve and get done. A parent, for example, has dozens of jobs: educator, taxi driver, chef, housekeeper, etc. as well as the jobs they are trying to do for themselves and their actual career. You may find you can bring a Dream Client's jobs into your marketing, to position yourself very differently to your competitors. Many of my clients, once they take a broader view of how they can use their marketing to connect with their Dream Clients, are able to use an understanding of their clients 'jobs' strategically, both to demonstrate shared values and that they possess a greater depth of understanding regarding their clients' lives. This builds a lot of goodwill and gratitude along the way, and is often used in 'side door marketing'.)

- Where would they like to be one year from now?

- Why is that important for them?

- How will it feel when they achieve their dream outcomes?

- What is stopping them from moving forward?

Explore these questions to start to understand your Dream Client and where they are today. You'll find the answers to these questions from speaking with them directly on sales calls, while networking, or in specific surveys or meetings. Once you've answered each question as fully as you can, review your answers to find the three biggest challenges your Dream Client faces that you feel you can (and want to) help them with.

Level Three: Defining Their Biggest Problems
Finally, for each of the three big problems you identified in Level Two, answer the following questions:

- How does your client know this is a problem for them? What are the signs?

- What is your client currently thinking about this problem and their ability to resolve it?

- In what way do they want to resolve it and in what time frame?

- What will a day in their life look and feel like once they resolve the problem, versus today?

- Why is resolving this issue important to them?

Reflect on your answers and note what they tell you about your Dream Client and how you can use your messaging, marketing and offers to deliver extraordinary value. In chapter four you'll map your client's journey. The information and insights you gain here will help you with both this exercise and the subsequent exercise, in chapter seven, where you'll turn your client's journey map into a high-impact, easy-to-implement marketing plan. So keep your answers safe!

Create your Dream Client Avatar

Now you've got to know your one Dream Client, create a one-page description of them. Add in as many details as possible. Give them a name and a face so they become real to you (and to your team if you have one). You may find that one of your existing clients perfectly represents your Dream Client's Avatar (DCA), in which case you can use their details for this exercise.

The goal is to become so clear who your Dream Client is that you could instantly recognise them if you were to meet them in person.

This happened to my client Helen.

When we started working together, Helen wasn't sure she had a viable business, let alone an idea of who she wanted to work with. But over the weeks, she fleshed out the details of her Dream Client and how she could serve them. She called her DCA Philip and found the perfect picture of him on Canva.com.

One week later, while networking, Philip walked in! As they spoke, he confirmed her first impressions. So, when Philip asked what she did, she was able to talk about her offer in a way that appealed to his needs and values. His response? 'Wow, that's just what I was looking for. Do you think we could work together?' Of course, Helen said yes, and over the next month she delivered her well-crafted confident speaker programme.

Philip was so happy with her programme and its results that he introduced Helen to his HR team so she could help more of the middle managers in their company. Within three months, Helen went from 'Could this work?', to booking her first corporate client. All because she took the time to really understand her Dream Client, and how she was uniquely placed to deliver exceptional value for them.

Your Red Flag List

Now you've defined your Dream Client, I want you to also define a nightmare client.

For this, you don't need to go into the same level of detail, but take some time to write down all the red flags that might indicate someone is likely to be a nightmare to work with.

This will help you avoid taking on clients who are more trouble than they're worth, giving you more time and energy to focus on your Dream Clients, business growth and to enjoy life.

Now you are clear on your True Value, who you most want to help, and the impact you want to create, the next step is to review this information to find your Value Sweet Spot – the space from which all your decisions and actions will have the most impact. So, if you're ready, it's time to grab your figurative tango shoes...

CHAPTER SUMMARY

- Where you start in business is never where you end up. Don't overthink your niche. Start where it makes sense to start right now and then adjust and evolve as you learn more about how you can use your True Value to make a difference in the world.

- Having a single clear niche can feel counterintuitive, but in reality it helps you stand out to your Dream Clients. It also allows you to focus your time and resources, enabling you to play a bigger game and have an impact you feel proud of. Spread yourself too thin and you'll struggle to attract clients and risk burning out.

- Marketing to a single Dream Client, rather than a 'niche', makes it easier to create messages, marketing and offers that are clear, compelling and personal, and that will resonate with your Dream Client.

Chapter Three

Your Value Sweet Spot

*Finding your Value Sweet Spot is
the key to a unique, profitable and
impactful business.*

You now have two important sets of information: everything that makes you *you*, your True Value; and everything about your ideal client, your Dream Client Avatar. Now it's time to do a bit of a tango to find where the two overlap. This is your Value Sweet Spot.

(Disclaimer: I have never danced the tango; however, when I watch it performed on *Strictly Come Dancing*, I'm always struck by how close and in sync the dancers are. It feels both precise and intuitive, and that's the vibe this part of the Value Whispering™ Process requires.)

Knowing your Value Sweet Spot helps you to make sense of all the information you've gathered so far, and to put it to use. Once you know how to use your True Value to positively impact your Dream Clients, you can remain focused on just those messages and activities that are meaningful and impactful. This will save you a lot of time, energy, money and frustration over the long term. It will also build your confidence, as you'll know you are creating the experience and results that you want for both you and your clients.

Knowing Your Value Sweet Spot Is Better Than Building Confidence

Focusing on what you do best, and how your existing awesomeness can create the most impact for others, naturally helps you to stand out. This is the ideal scenario – and it's exactly what happens when you know your Value Sweet Spot.

Your Value Sweet Spot is the unique overlap between what you do best, the difference it makes for your clients, and what your Dream Clients value most. It's the place where your skills, passions, and proven results meet your clients' real needs, making it easy for you to communicate your worth, stand out authentically, and attract the right opportunities. In short: your Value Sweet Spot is where your brilliance meets what your Dream Clients value most.

When you show up from that space, you will create the most impact for your Dream Client and marketplace – and without being loud, feeling pushy or changing anything about who you are or how you show up. All of your work will begin from and lead back to your own individual zone of genius; occupying this space, you won't just feel confident, but proud of the impact you create.

In my early thirties I became involved in a few women's networks. Having moved from London to Geneva, I saw that, while I had never felt held back in my career due to my gender, too many of my Swiss colleagues did. They hadn't benefited from the positive experiences and encouragement that I was fortunate to have received early in my career (listen to episode 196 of my podcast for more on this). As a result, these women had started to believe the message they'd heard once too often: 'You can't do that, you're a girl.'

I wanted to help change their beliefs, so I founded a women's network at the bank where I worked. Soon after, I was also invited to join the board of the Geneva Career Women's Forum. Over the two years that followed, I noticed something interesting. The biggest drive for women was not status, but contribution. When they felt they could add value and make a positive difference, they found it much easier to speak up, push for what they believed in and lead.

For me personally, when I am operating from my Value Sweet Spot, I know my views, ideas or experiences are meaningful and relevant, and as an introvert, this knowledge helps me to speak up more confidently and more often. I know I am making a contribution, and I am energised by this knowledge and motivated to provide more.

For most of my clients, once they have identified their Value Sweet Spot, communicating their value becomes natural. They start to show up differently and attract clients by being their true self, which in turn brings clarity, intention and confidence. As one client marvelled: 'I signed four new clients this week. I just spoke to them about what I do and why, and they signed up without even asking the price. I didn't even sell to them!' Of course, the truth was that she *did* sell to them; it's just that what most people think of as sales is bad sales. When sales is done well, it feels like a natural extension of what we do and how we create value for our clients. We'll cover sales conversations in detail in Chapter Nine.

When you show up and work from within your Value Sweet Spot, you recognise that no one else can do quite what you do, quite the way you do it. Suddenly the tendency to negatively compare yourself to others diminishes, and you step out of the loop of overthinking, and feeling that you are not good enough or in the wrong place (*hello, imposter syndrome*).

It becomes so much easier to get on, get out there and make your difference. Less wasted time and money; less overthinking, procrastination, and shiny object syndrome; more focus, impact and results. That's the power of the Value Sweet Spot.

And when you do more of the right things, and less of the things that fall outside your Value Sweet Spot, your work takes on a greater sense of meaning and purpose, bringing us nicely back to that sense of making a positive contribution. You start to feel more accomplished and fulfilled. You stop working *towards* fulfilling your potential and instead work *from* it. What if your big goals are not out there waiting for you in the distance, but here, right now, driving your every step? It's an exciting proposition.

In short, getting to know your Value Sweet Spot is where the real magic happens. Knowing it will make everything you do feel straightforward. Decisions become painless. Your messaging and marketing plan become easier to determine. Your sales process flows effortlessly from your first 'hello'. And the right people and opportunities become not just visible, but accessible. You start saying 'Yes' to more of the right things and 'No' to those that aren't a good fit, giving you more time, energy and focus. You set yourself on a virtuous path, and I can't wait to see where it takes you.

To give you some insight as to the results you can look forward to, I want to introduce you to Kate.

When I first started working with Kate, she described herself as a teacher who was "drowning in a sea of marketing woes," and believed this was holding back her business. But as we dug into her True Value, it soon became clear that Kate was so much more. She was a passionate educator with a unique philosophy focused on co-creating lessons that helped her young students become lifelong learners.

As her Value Sweet Spot became clear, so too did the reason her school had been struggling. When she spoke to potential clients, the way she talked about her lessons made her sound the same as her competitors. As a result, parents compared her with cheaper alternatives and chose the lowest priced option.

However, once Kate knew her Value Sweet Spot, she could express her value clearly and talk from the heart about the real difference her school made in the lives of her students. The change was instant. The very next parent who walked through the door signed their child up on the spot, despite Kate's higher fees. They finally understood the impact she offered and saw how closely her approach aligned with their own values and the future they wanted for their child.

Without defining her Value Sweet Spot, Kate would have continued to blend in and lose clients to inferior alternatives. Once she had a clear message and a deep understanding of her unique value, her school grew quickly. She welcomed more of her dream families to her school and, within six months, she was considering opening a second location to meet the rising demand.

Doing the Tango

So where do you begin your tango? I'm not sure how the judges of *Strictly Come Dancing* would rate my version of the much-loved dance, but here's the process I guide my clients through.

Take a piece of paper and draw a line down the middle. Then at the top of your left-hand column write 'My Value' and at the top of your right-hand column write 'My Dream Clients'. Then write your conclusions from the earlier exercises into the relevant columns. Review both lists, then underline and link the areas of your value that are most relevant to specific points in your Dream Client column.

Then answer the following questions:

- Why do I care about getting x result for my clients?

- What makes me the ideal choice for my Dream Clients?

- What makes my Dream Clients so perfect for me?

- What are our shared values?

Write out and reflect on your answers. Then complete the following table. There's an extended version of this in the book's resources at: www.melittacampbell.com/ValueWhisperingBook

Thing I can do for my client...	They'll love this because...	The positive difference it will make is...

Finding the Evidence

Now you know your Value Sweet Spot, there is just one more step: finding the evidence.

Once you know how you can stand out and create a meaningful impact, look for the proof of this in your past experiences, feedback and testimonials. Also, look back over your past successes and highlight the achievements or results that made you feel proud. Then assess exactly what you did to make those happen. Don't be modest here. You want to leave yourself in no doubt that you can work within your Value Sweet Spot and that, when you do, you will create magic!

As you and your business evolve, you may find your Value Sweet Spot evolves too. So, every six to twelve months, review this exercise to ensure the work you do and the messages you share are still fully aligned, so you can continue to create an impact you feel proud of.

Now you know your Value Sweet Spot, the next step is to weave this value through everything you do. But before you start, it's helpful to understand your client's journey, and how their needs and expectations evolve as they move closer to working with you. And that's what we'll cover next.

CHAPTER SUMMARY

- Your Value Sweet Spot is the unique overlap between what you do best, the difference it makes for your clients, and what your dream clients value most. It's where your skills, passions, and proven results meet your clients' real needs, making it easier to communicate your value, attract Dream Clients, and work with clarity, confidence, and impact.

- Operating from your Value Sweet Spot helps reduce overthinking, procrastination and comparison while increasing focus, fulfilment and results. Decisions become easier, messaging and marketing align naturally, you grow in confidence, and you show up for your Dream Clients consistently without being loud or pushy.

- Being clear on your Value Sweet Spot helps you create more effective offers, convert more prospects into high paying and satisfied clients, and makes your work more meaningful and fulfilling.

- You find your Value Sweet Spot by comparing your *True Value* with your *Dream Client Avatar*. Asking reflective questions helps you find the most relevant and impactful overlaps between these two. Review your Value Sweet Spot every six to twelve months to ensure it still aligns with your growth and evolving client needs.

Part Two

Value Weaving

*It's not how loudly you shout, but how
deeply you resonate.*

Now you know your True Value, you want to weave this through everything you think and do. What *you* uniquely offer should guide every decision you make and form the basis of all your messaging, marketing and sales processes. This way, without ever having to be loud or pushy, your True Value will shine through every interaction, including those with your future clients. You won't have to shout about what makes you different, because your Dream Clients, and everyone who comes close to you and your business, will *feel* your difference.

To begin weaving your value into your business, take the time to understand the steps your clients travel along in their journey towards working with you. By defining these steps, you'll be able to show up consistently, and by weaving your value throughout every stage, you will ensure a high level of service without over-extending yourself.

This is the key to steady and sustainable growth. Because at every step you engage exclusively with your Dream Client – and do not spread yourself thin trying to talk to everybody – success will follow faster than if you try to be the same, do the same and say the same as everyone else.

Put all of this together – this clarity, focus, flow and lack of internal resistance – and you'll find that this smooth, steady and thoughtful approach to business growth is accelerated and more impactful.

It all starts with mapping your client's journey. This is the framework that everything else hangs from. So let's start there.

Chapter Four

The Client Journey

Your messages and offers click into place once you know your Dream Clients' journey, and what resonates most for them at each distinct step.

When helping my clients map out their client journey, I encourage them to think of it like a flight of stairs.

When I was a child, my friends and I would often challenge each other to climb the stone steps home from school two or three steps at a time. It's not an easy or comfortable thing to do, and it often resulted in us going home with grazed knees – *again!* Needless to say, as an adult, I walk up every flight of stairs one step at a time. It's easier and far more comfortable. And that's the point. When you know your client's journey, you can create a series of steps that feel easy, comfortable and natural for them to take. And, as the old army saying goes: slow is smooth, and smooth is fast.

According to Chet Holmes in *The Ultimate Sales Machine*, only 3% of your audience is actively looking to buy, with up to another 7% considering it. This means that roughly 90% aren't ready to make a decision just yet. They're still working through key questions like:

- What's the real problem I'm experiencing?

- What are my options for solving it, and which feels right for me?

- What would a solution require in terms of time, money, and effort?

- Who can help me, and do I like and trust them?

These people may be curious, even interested in your offer, but they're not ready to commit to anything. That's why creating a thoughtful client journey matters. It gives potential clients the space, support, and insight they need to move forward at their own pace. Mapping your client journey helps you create marketing that focuses on long-term engagement with the broader audience, not just the small percentage ready to buy today. And in the long term, this gradual cultivation leads to more sales.

As with any relationship, clear communication is key to building understanding, trust and belief. And the key part of that communication is your True Value: when targeted correctly at your Dream Client, the clear expression of this True Value assures them that you get where they're coming from, and can help them reach where they want to go. Weave this through everything you say and reinforce your difference over time.

Your prospects will have many touchpoints with your business in the process of becoming a client, and each one will come at a specific stage in their journey towards a sales decision.

Awareness
The first step comes when your prospect becomes aware that they have a problem they would like to solve, and begins to actively search for solutions. They are not yet ready to buy into a specific solution, so

for this stage it's best to focus on providing content that helps them understand their problem, shows empathy for their situation, breaks down their options and helps objectively narrow down their choices.

At this stage, they will be asking themselves: 'What is my real problem and who provides what solution?' Then they will ask: 'Which solution feels most relevant to my problem the way I understand it?'

They will be taking in a lot of information from a range of sources, so ensure your content is clear, easy to follow and focused on answering these questions.

Consideration

Once they understand their problem, clients will actively start to look for ways to solve their problem and create a shortlist of vendors. At this stage they will be interested in more detail about what you do and why. They'll be asking themselves: 'Who do I like and trust to deliver what they promise?' At this point, it's helpful to create content that highlights how your offer solves their problem, explains the 'why' behind your solution, and provides a high-level and brief overview of your offer.

Decision

By this stage, potential clients will be clearer on the solution that feels right for them, and they will be actively deciding which vendor to choose. Their big questions now will be: 'Do I like this offer and trust that it will solve my problem in a way that fits my needs and values?' and 'Is now the right time for me to invest in this solution?'

This is the time to put more time and energy into the relationship. Depending on the price point of your offer, this will typically involve a sales conversation for higher-ticket offers, or a detailed sales page for lower ticket offers.

Retention

Your new client will stay with you as long as you continue to solve their problem and make them feel valued. A good onboarding process that further embeds your True Value will help with this, as will client care throughout your relationship. Like a good customer care agent, it's good to regularly ask your client: 'Is there anything else I can do to help you?' This will keep you focused on their needs and highlight any further opportunities to support them (and grow your business in the process).

Advocacy

Those clients who have enjoyed working with you, and value the results you've helped them achieve, will be more than happy to recommend you to others. Referrals from clients are gold, as any referred prospect usually has a good impression of you before even meeting you.

But referrals aren't always automatic. Many people don't think to make them or aren't sure if you'd even want them to. And even if they do realise the value of a referral, they might not know how to go about making one.

So be sure to actively ask for referrals and offer clients support in making them. A suitable moment is directly after they have shown you some appreciation. Seize the opportunity with a simple enquiry like: 'I'm so pleased you are getting such great results from our work together. I would love to help more people like you to [insert result]. Do you know a another [insert a short description of your Dream Client] who might also appreciate these kinds of results?'

When you receive a referral, thank the referrer and keep them updated. If you do, they may well refer you to more people in the future. If you don't, they usually won't.

Nurturing Your Prospects and Clients through the Client Journey

How you nurture your prospective clients will change as they move along this client journey sequence. For example, at the Awareness stage, you shouldn't invest too much time in each individual relationship, as your prospect is a long way from becoming a client and may never become one at all.

At this stage, it can be easy to overwhelm your client with too much information, which may leave them feeling pressured or, worse, confused. A confused mind doesn't buy or buy into anything. So take your time and keep things clear and simple, and signpost the way to the next level of information so they can take this next step once they are ready.

As the client moves closer to working with your business, you can take the conversation progressively deeper. Remember, it's uncomfortable to run up more than one step at a time, so take your time, break things down, and focus on creating a smooth, enjoyable and logical journey. Even if you see your competitors attempting to set up quicker sales and onboarding processes, don't assume this is working. I've often had prospects approach me because another business coach made them feel bad or pressured.

When deciding on your best steps, keep your Value Sweet Spot in mind to ensure that all your decisions fall within your zone of genius and will be meaningful and impactful for your audience.

Mapping Your Client Journey

By creating a simple map of your client journey, you will start to understand the different ways you should frame your messaging at each stage. To do this, create five columns on a page, and follow these instructions.

First column: write each of the client journey stages detailed above.

Second column: write down the typical questions or challenges your Dream Clients will have at each stage. AI can help you brainstorm this, using prompts like 'Act as a [add your Dream Client avatar]. What are twenty questions or challenges you have when trying to [add in the problem your Dream Client is trying to solve]?' Review the answers and add them to your list when you feel they're accurate.

Third column: write down everything you do that answers these questions or resolves these challenges. And in a different colour, note your ideas of what else you *could* do, or what you could do differently.

Fourth column: write down what you want your prospects to think, feel and do as a result of each of the answers or activities you've listed in the third column.

Fifth column: note down what you feel you do well and what, if anything, you could improve.

Sixth column: write down how you will know a particular message or activity is working. What will you see happen if it works as you expect?

Once you have your completed map, assess how well your content and activities flow from one stage to another. You may have listed the same activity under more than one stage – that's fine. But assess how it serves the various stages differently.

Finally, consider what activities and messaging you can realistically manage, and courageously strip anything else out. The goal in business isn't to do all the things and burn out, but to focus on a small number of actions that work well and have the desired impact. Regularly checking on the effectiveness of your activities will help you to remain streamlined, impactful and sane as you build and grow your business over time.

Once you have your completed Client Journey Map, you have the first stage of your marketing plan. How exciting is that! All you need to do is take the actions from your third column, break these down into smaller actions, and then plan when you will take these and in what order. Ta da!

To help you with this exercise, I have created a Client Journey Map template that you can download for free. The template contains a completed example and a short video to help guide you. You can download it for free at: www.melittacampbell.com/ValueWhisperingBook

Tracking Client Progress

Your Client Journey Map should be a living tool that helps drive consistent business growth. Track your client's journey — are all your activities working as you expected? If you are not seeing the outcomes you've listed in the fifth column of your map, avoid the temptation to get more aggressive and push people into action. Instead, explore what can be improved. In particular, check your messaging, is it speaking directly to your dream client? Nine times out of ten, that's where the issue lies, and small tweaks can make a big difference.

Staying focused on what works frees up your time — time you

can then focus on hot prospects (those at the decision stage) and paying clients. Spending time here will give you the highest return on investment.

As you learn more about your clients, and as your business evolves, keep your Client Journey Map and marketing plan updated. But for now, you are ready to move on to the next stage: creating an irresistible offer.

CHAPTER SUMMARY

- Creating a Client Journey Map helps you to understand your prospects' changing needs as they go from discovering they have a problem, to choosing your service to help them solve it. This understanding is the basis of a simple and effective marketing plan.

- A series of small logical steps that guide your customer through their client journey will yield better and faster results than a process with a few big leaps.

- Once you have mapped your client journey, assess everything to ensure it is simple, effective and manageable. Assess and update this regularly, especially as you learn more about what works best.

Chapter Five

Creating an Irresistible Offer

Your offer is the ultimate expression of your True Value, a powerful catalyst for positive change.

Your offer is how you guide your client from where they are today – stuck and disheartened – to a place where their problem no longer causes friction in their lives. When your offer is situated within your Value Sweet Spot, you will be in a strong position to create a perfect solution for your Dream Client, one that is unlike anything else in the market. Your offer is the ultimate expression of your True Value and a powerful catalyst for positive change.

As discussed in the previous chapter, your Dream Client is unlikely to immediately invest in your core programme. This does sometimes happen, but it's the exception not the rule. It's more likely that someone will take the time to get to know you and your solution, decide if they like and trust you, and then enquire about working with you. Creating a series of offers – an offer ecosystem – can help lead them along this process.

Your Offer Sequence

An offer ecosystem helps guide prospects to your one Core Offer, serving them more deeply than your messaging and marketing alone can do. Your ecosystem can also continue to serve them *after* they have finished your Core Offer.

Your offer sequence should fit neatly into the Customer Journey Map you worked on in the previous chapter. Here's an example of what this sequence may look like. I would recommend that you start with this sequence, then build on or adapt it over time as you learn more about your Dream Clients and how you can best deliver value.

1) Your Free Offer

When I was a child, my school friends and I would go around the playground shouting, 'Whoever wants to play hopscotch, follow on!' Anyone wanting to play with us would hold on to the waist of the last person in the line, and we'd snake around the playground until we had enough people to play.

This is what your Free Offer should do. Call out to your clients, 'Whoever has this problem and wants to solve it, follow on.' At the Awareness and Consideration stages of the customer journey, this allows promising prospects to identify themselves.

Just like a child's game, your Free Offer should be easy to join in. Create a simple landing page (a standalone webpage with no navigation bar, only a form requiring a name and email address), and once you have received a prospect's information, make sure your Free Offer delivers its promised value quickly and simply. Ensure this value is linked to your Core Offer, so those people who request it are also likely to be interested in working with you more deeply down the line.

Crucially, also ensure that your Free Offer is deliverable at scale at a low cost and with minimal effort. As we are still early in the customer journey process, we must remember that the majority of prospects won't progress to paying clients. As Google Think highlighted in a 2024 study: "capturing shoppers' attention doesn't necessarily mean you've captured their business"[2].

At the Awareness and Consideration stages, your prospects aren't always paying full attention to you, so make good use of the email address they have provided. Follow up regularly, adding value to the relationship and building the trust needed for you to be seen as their ideal choice. A value-driven automated email sequence is ideal here. And in all your emails, be sure to clearly signpost your messaging pertaining to the next step of the customer journey, for those ready to take it.

The key to creating a highly attractive Free Offer is to 1) keep it focused on your Dream Client's biggest problem (see the work you did in chapter two); and 2) make it the first step towards your new prospect understanding the value of your Core Offer. For that reason, while the offers are listed here in client-journey order, you might find it easier to design your offer sequence in the opposite order: starting with your Core Offer, followed by your Bridging Offer, with your Free Offer last.

It's easy to overthink your Free Offer. To avoid this, if possible I recommend that you create your Free Offer from some of your existing content. Take one small piece of your Core Offer – for example, a signature webinar – and turn this into a guide, checklist, tip sheet, swipe file, mini masterclass, etc. It will not only save you time, but ensure your Free Offer is focused on solving your client's problem.

To help you get started, I've included a list of Free Offer ideas in the resources page that accompanies this book. You'll find that at: www.melittacampbell.com/ValueWhisperingBook

---

2   https://www.thinkwithgoogle.com/consumer-insights/consumer-trends/increase-full-fun-nel-conversions/

2) Your Bridging Offer

Staying with our playground analogy, think back to the friends you had at school. You were probably reasonably good friends with many of your classmates — except that mean kid who pulled your hair! But you likely had a smaller number of close friends who *really* understood you, the ones who liked and wanted the same things. And I bet many of those kids went from classmate to BFFs through some kind of shared experience that helped you see how much you had in common.

That's the kind of experience you want to create with your Bridging Offer. You want it to provide that first taste of working together, so that you can find out which of your new leads share your values, relate to your perspective, have a problem you can help solve, and appreciate the way you show up and share value.

A Bridging Offer is a chance for your Dream Clients to step forward. You should give your new prospect more value and deepen the relationship you've started, telling them more about your unique solution and previewing the experience of working towards it.

Your Bridging Offer will typically be free or low cost, although this will ultimately depend on your industry and the price point of your Core Offer.

Aim to create a simple experience that will surprise and delight your prospects, one you can offer to multiple people at a time so it can be delivered consistently, at low cost and scale.

Bridging Offers are great at the Consideration stage of the customer journey, as they allow your prospects to understand your offer and its value by interacting with you directly. Any questions they have, you can answer; any doubts, you can address.

Demonstrations of your product or tool, audits, webinars, workshops, mini-courses, and events are all good Bridging Offers, but this list is far from exhaustive. Be creative with how you can help your client get an accurate and enticing taste of what they stand to gain from your Core Offer. And as always, keep your Value Sweet Spot in mind so you can create something you'll enjoy delivering.

It is sometimes a challenge to come up with an offer that doesn't repeat the content of your Core Offer. But you don't need to worry about that. In fact, if you do use a small part of your Core Offer as your Bridging Offer, you will know those people who liked it will also like the full package. And since your Bridging Offer is just a small part of the bigger picture, your Core Offer will still add a lot of value.

Take this book, for example. It is low cost and gives the reader (you), a step-by-step breakdown of most of my Value Whispering™ Blueprint (my Core Offer). However, if you were to join my Value Whispering™ Blueprint programme, there would be the further value of my personal feedback, advice, support and accountability every step of the way. The Bridging Offer contains part of the Core Offer, but the Core Offer remains a different, more complete, and a much more valuable experience.

But that is not to say that the book is a *lesser* offer. In fact, it contains something that the Core Offer does not, and this is a result of its low cost and its placement within the customer journey process. This book offers a minimal-commitment opportunity for you to verify that you relate to my way of seeing business growth. By the end of the book, you will be far more informed as to the kind of value I offer and its worth to you. You will be ready to proceed along your own customer journey with a greater understanding and a deeper frame of reference – regardless of whether you decide to get in contact for more information, hire me immediately, or decide to pursue other service providers/solutions.

That is the unique value of the Bridging Offer.

Your Core Offer

Your Core Offer is the main event. It is like that special game you and your best friends used to play, when everyone was all-in, understanding all the rules and fully immersed in the fun. For me, a favourite pastime was creating a showjumping course around my house, where my friends and I would leap over obstacles, pretending we were riding our favourite horses.

Remember to base your Core Offer on your Value Sweet Spot. This ensures that the solution you offer draws on your personality, values and strengths. You'll also be able to use your time and energy where they can have most impact, without overextending yourself, and still create an exceptional experience to stand out in your market.

You want to be courageous and bold with your Core Offer. You know what it takes to free your Dream Client from their problem, and they do not. They may *say* they do, but if that were true, they wouldn't be looking for your help in the first place. Trust your own expertise and break down the steps you believe they need to take to get the best outcomes. Then create your Core Offer around that.

Consider four things as you do so.

1. What steps does a client need to take to get to the stage where their problem is solved?

2. At each step of this process, what do they need to think, feel and do in order to progress to the next step?

3. What tools, training, guidance, etc. do they need to guide them towards these thoughts, feelings and actions?

4. What is the best way to deliver this value? For example, if your Dream Client is a young parent, your delivery method will be very different than if your client is a senior leader, or retired couple – even if the problem to be solved is the same.

As you start to take clients through your Core Offer, pay attention to what works and what doesn't. Engage your clients in discussions to learn their perspectives on the process, so you can keep refining and improving your offer to deliver exceptional results. Your first clients could be more accurately seen as co-creators, helping you to shape and improve your offer.

If you notice that some clients get extraordinary results, while others get only OK results, see if you can pinpoint a difference in their behaviours, then incentivise those behaviours. For example, when I first started running the Value Whispering™ Blueprint programme, I noticed that the clients who got the best results were those who asked a lot of questions and regularly asked for feedback. So I amended the programme to include private sessions at key points, to ensure that all my clients got the depth of insight and support they needed to succeed beyond their expectations. And currently, I'm creating custom AI tools to help guide my clients through those parts of the process that are most frequently reported as time-consuming, or where I've noticed more clients tend to overthink.

Follow-On Offers

Even the best games come to a natural conclusion. But that doesn't mean that the fun has to end. It's just time to play a different game. After our energetic show jumping games, my horse-mad friends and I would rest together watching *The Black Stallion* (again) while guzzling a giant bag of Butterkist popcorn.

Since the most expensive and time-consuming part of your marketing is the acquisition of new clients, you want to maximise the value of each client by 1) keeping them as a paying client as long as possible; and 2) encouraging them to refer their friends and acquaintances to you. This will help you stay profitable and continue helping people over the long term.

To keep clients beyond your Core Offer, you want to have at least one Follow-On Offer. This should extend the value you provide in a way they love and appreciate. What will they need after they have solved their biggest problem? Are there other, related problems that they need help with? Do they need support to maintain the results of your Core Offer?

Since you want to put most of your energy and resources into your Core Offer, your Follow-On Offer should be something of high value to your clients, but low cost and effort for you. One of the easiest ways to determine the right Follow-On Offer is to simply ask each client: 'Is there anything else I can help you with?' Or look to what others are doing for inspiration — and not just those in your industry, but in other industries too.

For example, once they finish my programme, Blueprinters (the name my clients gave themselves) are offered the chance to join my Alumni Offer. By this stage, their fundamental questions about their business and marketing have been replaced with deeper questions about their business growth, which we explore during long monthly calls. The value for my clients is high, but the amount of effort required on my side is less than the twice-weekly calls of my core programme.

Naming Your Offers

The final stage is to give your offers names. It's worth starting with the Core Offer and then seeing if this establishes a pattern you can use across all your offers. It doesn't always work out this way, but it's nice when it does.

There are few rights or wrongs when it comes to choosing a name, but here are some pointers to help guide your thinking and eventual choice:

- Focus your name on the benefits of your offer. In other words, after working with you, what will your clients be able to do and enjoy that they can't today? This will give your name an aspirational quality. For example: 'Become Fully Booked in 90 Days'.

- Include reference to your client or their characteristics, so that your title naturally calls them out. For example: 'The Busy Parents Productivity Plan'.

- Make your name plainly descriptive of what's on offer. For example: 'VIP Marketing Strategy Day'.

- Reference your unique solution, brand or True Value. For example: The Value Whispering™ Blueprint. You can then trademark your name to protect it.

- Have a slightly cryptic name that piques curiosity, then explain more in the tagline and messaging. For example: 'The Quiet Advantage, Turn your introverted strengths into a powerful marketing strategy.'

An AI tool like ChatGPT can be a great help with brainstorming. Try this prompt to help you get started: 'Act as a brand strategist. I [insert offer details]. Please suggest ten offer names that are aspirational, benefit-led, and aligned with a [insert appropriate] tone.' To help your 'brand strategist' generate even more tailored results, you can also include your desired offer outcomes, client type, and brand tone of voice in the prompt.

Once you have your name, do a Google search it to see if it is already being used by another business. If so, find an alternative name – this will help you stand out and save you possible legal complications later. If you don't find anything on Google, also check Amazon and YouTube. Finally, if it all looks good, check if your name is available as a domain name on GoDaddy or Register.com. This search won't take you long, but could save you a lot of effort, fines and heartache further down the line.

Now you know your Dream Client, Your Value Sweet Spot and you have your offers, it's time to nail down your messaging. Your message will express your True Value in a way that attracts your Dream Clients and keeps them moving happily and smoothly through their customer journey. This is a crucial step. People don't buy the best solution; they buy the solution they best understand.

Despite this, communicating the value of their offers is the thing many business owners find hardest. And if your business is you, it can feel even more weird and awkward. But by combining the steps in the next chapter with the work you've already done, you will find that communicating your value is more straightforward than you might realise.

CHAPTER SUMMARY

- Create a simple sequence of offers designed to gently guide your prospects towards your Core Offer, filtering out those who don't match your Dream Client criteria along the way.

- Keep your Value Sweet Spot front of mind as you design your offers. This will ensure your work becomes a true expression of your value and a catalyst for positive change for your clients.

- Assess and tweak your offers and nurturing processes over time as you learn what works best and what behaviours makes certain clients more successful.

- Give your offers names but check them thoroughly before proceeding further, to ensure they aren't in use by other businesses and that they are available as domain names and for trademarking.

Chapter Six

Your Core Message

*Talking about your business can feel
weird and awkward, until you can do it
with clarity, intention and heart.*

There will be many messages you share with your audience over the lifetime of your business. But they all should stem from your Core Message – the message that simply and plainly explains what you are all about.

Your Core Message tells the world what you do, who you help and why you care. And the good news is that, in Chapters One, Two and Three, you have already gathered the information you need to create it. All you need to do now is identify it and give it some structure.

Your Core Message, coupled with the right offers, will do a lot of the heavy lifting for you when it comes to turning prospects into happy, paying clients. When your marketing is built around a clear Core Message, those prospects who advance to the Decision stage of the customer journey will believe you offer the value and solution they seek, before they've even talked to you directly.

You'll find you barely have to sell yourself further, if at all. Instead, you'll simply need to verify the prospects' needs and confirm if your offer is the right choice for them right now. Your sales conversations will feel enjoyable to both you and your prospect, no pushy tactics required. We'll cover sales conversations in depth in chapter eight.

Getting your Core Message right can take time. When you have expertise and experience built from years of study and practice, explaining what you do can feel complicated. And if that's how you feel, I've got your back. The steps in this chapter will help you find and express your True Value through one core message suite.

But your Core Message is not your *only* message. Over time you'll add to it, maybe even qualify it. But having a Core Message will help you keep those subsequent messages consistent and coherent as your business grows.

I like to break a Core Message down into three components that will make up your Core Message suite:

1. Your Brand Story: Why you do what you do (and for whom).

2. Your Signature System: How you deliver your service uniquely.

3. Your WAW Factor: The positive results and impact you create.

As you move through this chapter, you may find yourself doubting your right to stand up and say: 'I'm great at this!' Sometimes it is difficult to remember your successes, and all too easy to picture your struggles and failures along the way. When we look to the future, to the life we want to create for ourselves, sometimes this only makes us feel how far away we are from that success.

In other words, it's hard to see the wood for the trees. But as you work through this chapter, I want you to trust that you are exactly where you need to be right now; to bravely put any doubts to the side. Show any negative thoughts gratitude – after all, they are just trying to keep you safe – and then with kindness invite them to sit this one out. We'll explore the topic of mindset further in chapter eleven.

With that said, it's time to create a message you can share with ease, pride and impact. Follow these six steps to identify the key information to include in your Core Message, and start to give this a structure that will position you as your Dream Clients' ideal choice.

Step 1: Creating Your Brand Story

For this step, you need to explore *why* you do what you do.

This can be challenging. You may have started your business for reasons that feel more selfish than inspiring. For example, when I started my communication consultancy, my initial objective was simply to earn some money and 'keep my hand in' while I took time away from my career to raise my young family. But the message 'I launched my business to get your money' would not attract or inspire anyone. I needed a public-facing 'why'.

And looking deeper, I soon found it. I had seen firsthand how, when companies and leaders communicated well with their employees and stakeholders, they had a positive impact on internal culture, happiness, fulfilment and profitability. And I wanted to help more companies and leaders to experience this impact. That was my public-facing 'why'.

But while you want your public-facing 'why' to inspire your Dream Client, you can still use your personal 'why' to inform your choice of business model and the way you structure and deliver your offers.

Here's how to find your public-facing 'why':

1. Start by brainstorming or journalling all the reasons why you started your business – both your personal and public-facing ideas (you may prefer to keep these on two separate lists). Then highlight the ones that you feel most connected to, before narrowing your final choice down to just one option. You may be unable to decide your final 'why' between several

different points. Don't let this stop you. Pare the list down to the fewest possible entries and move on. The subsequent steps will likely help you narrow this down further.

2. Next, think about your vision. How would you love the world to be different thanks to your work? It can be helpful to think about what you love or hate to see happen for your clients. Picture how the lives of your clients could be different if more people had access to your knowledge, tools and support. You may find tools like journalling, meditation or tapping (Emotional Freedom Technique) helpful here. You want to free your mind to think big.

3. Look back to your True Value. How does that influence what you do and how? Why will your clients love this about you and your work? How does it make you different or better than your competitors?

4. Reflect on all your answers and pull them together into one brand story: a narrative that communicates how you got to where you are today, the lessons you learned along the way, and how you now use this experience to benefit your clients. You may find it helpful to follow these steps:

    a. Brainstorm everything you can think of that relates to your story: childhood dreams and experiences, education, hobbies, work, best/worst moments, awards, etc. Don't try and create polished stories; bullet points are fine at this stage. In particular, hone in on your aha! moments, the moments when something suddenly made sense.[3]

---

3   Keep your original list safe. It will be invaluable for inspiring social media posts, articles and emails.

b.	Go back through your points and highlight those elements that are most relevant/relatable to your ideal client.

c.	Organise the elements you've highlighted into a logical story. This doesn't always have to be chronological. If it enhances your story, reinforces a point and flows well, you can include client stories within your own story too. E.g. 'I can remember the first time a client got x result…'

d.	Write out your story and set it aside. Then review it after a day (or more) and edit your text. Put yourself in the shoes of your ideal client: is everything meaningful, relevant and interesting to them?

e.	Ask at least one other person to read your story and tell you how it feels to them. What are the key messages they take away? Do they have any questions? If possible, find someone who is representative of your ideal client.

You may wonder how long your brand story should be. And it's a good question. There is no one ideal length; in fact, it can be helpful to have a few versions of differing lengths ready to use in different situations. But I recommend you keep it as concise as possible without losing the intended meaning. And whatever length you opt for, keep this classic copywriting wisdom in mind: 'There's no such thing as too long, just too boring.'

5.	Finally, consider any client stories and testimonials that back up your brand story and speak to the value and impact you create. Then use them in your marketing to provide social proof of your ability to get results for your Dream Clients. People like to see that others have achieved results by working with you. It makes their decision to buy feel much less risky. Not to mention that collecting such testimonials helps build and maintain your self-belief.

Step 2: Creating your Signature System

Have you ever been asked what you do and found yourself struggling to give a clear answer? For many business owners, the honest response is often, 'Well… it's complicated.'

Other times, it's not that what you do is complicated, but that you have so much expertise you don't know where to begin. Years of expertise and experience mean you could talk for hours. But while your answer might be truthful, that doesn't mean it's clear, or that the person you're talking to will stay engaged long enough to hear it all.

As I said earlier, a confused mind doesn't buy or buy into anything. That's why you need to be able to explain the journey on which you take your clients in a way that's simple, clear and easy to follow. Your Signature System does exactly that. It's a step-by-step process that shows your Dream Client how you take them from feeling stuck, lost or frustrated, to feeling clear, in control and confident about their future.

Your Signature System is unique to you. It's based on your expertise, experience, values and preferred way of working. It's the essence of your True Value. It gives you a repeatable process for creating consistent, predictable results you can be proud of and that your Dream Clients love. It also helps you stand out, standardise much of your content and approach, and save time, energy and resources.

Start by breaking your work down into three to five key milestones. These are the stages your Dream Client moves through from the moment they start working with you, right through to their dream outcome. If you have more than five milestones, see if you can group some together.

To find these milestones, answer the following:

1. **Where are your clients when they first start working with you?** What's their situation, challenge or mindset?

2. **What's the first milestone they need to reach?** What do they need to do, think or feel differently to get there? What happens when they arrive at this stage?

3. **Repeat this process for each subsequent milestone** until you've mapped the full journey.

For each stage, consider:

- **The problem** they have at this point.

- **The progress** they'll make: the steps, tools and guidance you'll provide to move them forward.

- **The promise:** what they'll walk away with when they complete that stage.

It is easy to get carried away when listing the milestones. Beware of this. Three to five is really the sweet spot. When I first started training communication professionals, when planning what to teach, I listed fifty-three things they needed to know to communicate effectively. But I soon realised I couldn't teach fifty-three things in a one-day workshop, so I started to group and combine them. I ended up with my *Four Golden Rules of Impactful Communication* — four rules that, fifteen years later, still stand true. Sometimes, less is more.

As you define your milestones, name each one. These names should ideally hint at both *what* the step involves and the *outcome* it delivers. This is how I created the steps of my Value Whispering™ Blueprint: Value Understanding, Value Weaving and Self-Leadership.

Finally, name your Signature System. Often the most relevant name will emerge naturally from the milestone names. Keep the focus on clarity, the 'what' and the outcome.

This system will sit at the heart of all your communications. Your business pitch, sales conversations, articles, podcast interviews, signature talk... They should all articulate and name your Signature System.

You can listen to episode 205 of my podcast, *The Art of Value Whispering*, to hear me talking about creating your Signature System. It's a powerful and flexible tool, and one of my favourite business communication techniques.

When my client Sam tried to map out the milestones in her Signature System, she hit a roadblock. An expert in natural fertility and pregnancy with significant experience, she knew her work inside out, but as no two clients ever took exactly the same path, she found it challenging to find one 'system' that underpinned her work. However, as we talked, one truth emerged: every woman she worked with shared the same need. To be heard.

Sam realised her process always began by listening deeply to her clients' needs, desires and challenges, allowing these women their voices. She realised that her Signature System was the way she listened, organised her clients' needs and created a bespoke plan for each one.

When she started to map out this process, she realised that it had five distinct steps that spelt out 'VOICE'. The realisation gave me goosebumps! Now, with her VOICE system clear, she could explain her work in one compelling sentence: 'I give women a VOICE when deciding on the fertility and pregnancy journey they want to take.'

It's memorable, meaningful and positions her instantly as the expert.

When you have a Signature System, you stop saying 'It's complicated' and start communicating with confidence and clarity.

You become known for the transformation you deliver, and your prospects can see exactly how they'll get from where they are to where they want to be. It expresses your True Value *and* the transformation your clients walk away with. This quickly answers every prospect's first and biggest question: 'What's in it for me?'

Which neatly brings us to the final element of your Core Message suite...

Step 3: What they Walk Away With (the WAW Factor)

The first and biggest question every prospect has is: 'What's in it for me?' They want to quickly understand what they will **W**alk **A**way **W**ith after working with you.

Your brand story and signature system help build credibility and trust, and establishes your True Value in the prospect's mind. But clients ultimately pay you for the results they walk away with, so this needs to be clear and distinct. That's where the WAW Factor comes in.

What will your clients be able to do after your collaboration that they can't do today, and how will that impact the quality of their future? It's vital to make your WAW Factor message simple and clear, and to share it quickly in your conversations. You want it to be one sentence that prospects can easily remember.

It's not always easy, especially when you are selling an intangible service. But it is always possible.

Here are some questions to help you identify your WAW Factor:

1. What do your clients walk away with after working with you? How do they look, feel, think or act differently? What does this enable them to achieve that they can't do today? Why is this important to them?

2. How does your WAW Factor address their problem?

3. How does this outcome fit with their goals, dream, preferences and values?

As always, free-write your answers and then review and regroup your answers until you find the one most powerful WAW Factor. But keep all your other ideas safe, as you can use these to inspire additional marketing content later on.

When you have your WAW Factor message, test it out as often as possible to help you refine and improve it. Networking conversations are a great way to do this, especially if you are attending an event where you can speak with lots of people in quick succession, to refine your message quickly and in real time.

Bringing it all Together

You now have a powerful pitch on your hands that you can use in any situation. Here's how it all fits together:

Open with your brand story. This shows why you care and creates an emotional connection with your audience or prospect.

Then share your Signature System, to add credibility and logic.

End with your WAW Factor sentence. This is the final piece that will lead your Dream Clients to say: 'OMG I *NEED* this!'

By bringing all the elements together in this way, you will step by step build the belief someone needs to buy from you: first they will get to know you; then they will come to like you; then they will learn to trust you and believe that you can deliver what you promise. You will have positioned yourself as an experienced, caring authority in your niche, with a unique offer that gets results.

Using Your Core Message

Condense your Core Message into three or four short paragraphs that you can memorise and use in any situation to explain what you do. Use this on the homepage of your website, your social media profiles, and as your introduction while networking or public speaking.

For longer pitches and podcast interviews, you can use the same structure, but layer in further personal stories, client case studies and relevant facts and figures.

You may be tempted to switch up your Core Message every now and again, so people don't get bored of hearing the same message. Resist this temptation! Before people buy from you, they need to know, like, and trust you, and believe your solution is the best way to solve their problem. It's the repetition of your Core Message that builds this recognition and trust (and your ability to confidently express your value in any situation). Remember you are the only person who sees every message you create; your audience only ever sees a small percentage.

Your Core Message isn't just useful for external communication — it's also a powerful internal tool. It helps your team, partners, and service providers stay aligned with what you do, why you do it, and how. In this way, you can protect your culture as you grow. When new team members, freelancers, or collaborators are familiar with your Core Message, they're far more likely to keep it front of mind as they make decisions, helping to carry your vision forward with consistency.

CHAPTER SUMMARY

- Your Core Message suite is made up of three essential parts:

  1. Your Brand Story (why you do what you do)

  2. Your Signature System (how you deliver results)

  3. Your WAW Factor (the impact you create).

- Your Core Message explains what you do, who you help, and why you care. It captures the heart of your value and work in a way others, especially your Dream Clients, can instantly understand and relate to.

- When your message is clear and paired with the right offers, it does much of the hard work for you, drawing in the right people and helping them see your value before you even speak. And when you do speak, it helps convert prospects into paying clients.

- It's completely normal for crafting and refining your Core Message to take time, especially when your expertise runs deep.

- Once you've shaped your Core Message suite, you can tailor it to fit any format – your website, social bio or networking intro. You can also expand your Core Message to give you a solid framework for talks, podcasts and webinars.

- Internally, your Core Message helps your team stay aligned and consistent as you grow. When everyone is on the same page from the start, it's easier to protect your culture and purpose.

Chapter Seven

Marketing Made Simple

You don't have to be loud to market your business, stand out and make a positive difference.

A couple of years ago I was scrolling through a Facebook group for female founders when I read a post that made my jaw drop. This is what it said:

> 'Six months ago I decided to stop marketing my business. Instead, I started showing up as myself and focused on delivering exceptional value for my niche, and guess what – now I'm getting clients!'

I was horrified. Who on earth told this lady that being yourself and adding value wasn't marketing?!

Marketing (and sales for that matter) has nothing to do with being fake, pushy or manipulative. It's not about wasting people's time with a load of hot air and baloney. And it's not about boastful self-promotion or 'scratching the pain until it bleeds and then selling the Band Aid'. It's about adding value, starting meaningful relationships based on trust and understanding, and it's about deeply serving your clients with thoughtfully designed products and services that will transform their lives in a positive way.

In this chapter, I'm going to break that process down for you so you can comfortably and successfully market your business, attract the right people and opportunities, and have an impact you feel proud of. As ever, the first step is to be yourself; you cannot successfully attract the right people and opportunities into your life if you are being anyone else.

But before we dive in, I want to quickly recap the elements of marketing we have already covered in this book. Revisiting this toolkit will make the work in this chapter, and beyond, easier.

Your True Value: In Chapter One you identified and embraced your True Value, all the learning and experiences that have shaped who you are today.

Your Dream Clients: In Chapter Two you identified your perfect-fit clients and started to learn more about the world they live in, the problems they face, and how they would like to solve these problems.

Your Value Sweet Spot: In Chapter Three you looked at where your True Value overlaps with the needs and aspirations of your Dream Clients. This is the space where you can naturally stand out and make the biggest difference, while staying focused, productive and happy.

Your Client Journey: In Chapter Four, you looked at the steps your Dream Client takes to arrive in your world, and how their questions and needs evolve as they take each subsequent step towards solving their big problem.

Your Offer: In Chapter Five, you looked at how you can create an offer for your Dream Clients that is a powerful catalyst for positive change, and how a simple sequence of offers can help your prospect buy into your Core Offer.

Your Core Message: In Chapter Six, you started to create a simple suite of messages that can work together in any situation to marry the emotional appeal of your solution with the logic behind why it works.

In this chapter, you'll start to bring all of this together into a simple plan, one that will put you in front of your Dream Clients on a consistent basis, and encourage them to take the all-important step of booking a sales conversation or visiting your sales page. That is the moment you can really start to transform their lives and guide them to the results they desire.

Marketing is all about putting the client and their needs at the centre of every decision you make. And using your Value Sweet Spot to guide all your decisions takes this even further, ensuring that everything you provide for your clients aligns perfectly with your strengths, supports your desired lifestyle, and ensures you deliver results in a way that's unique to you and your business.

That's how you naturally stand out – without shouting.

Mapping Your Marketing Plan to Your Client Journey

You already have your client journey mapped out. Now all you need to do is add in an extra column, and determine the activities needed at each step to move the prospect along to the following step. This is your high-level marketing plan.

For example, at the first stage – Awareness – most people will only just be starting to recognise they have a problem they'd like to solve. They will have lots of questions about their problem, why it occurred, and how they might resolve it. In other words, they will be thirsty for information, but they will not yet be ready to commit to a solution.

If this is true for your prospects, brainstorm all the ways you could provide this information. Leaflets, brochures, posters, newsletters, blog posts, podcast episodes, emails, social media content, eBooks, checklists, templates, videos, webinars, public speaking, advertising, magazine articles, direct conversations, infographics, reports, white papers... Think broadly and write down as many as you can. Don't discount anything at this stage; anything goes. You can ask your preferred AI tool to help generate ideas, but you should always verify them yourself.

Review your list and 1) underline in one colour all those activities that could reach many people at the same time. Remember, at this stage, your prospects are an eclectic bunch, and they have yet to demonstrate they are open to what you have to offer; you don't want to waste time and money chasing individuals.

Next 2) in a second colour underline all those activities that you feel you are ready and able to do and that you would enjoy.

Next 3) in a third colour underline those activities which align with the ways you think (or ideally know) your Dream Clients prefer

to receive information. If you are not yet familiar with your clients'
preferences, make an educated guess and then test it out. Did you get
the response you wanted? If not, simply try something else.

And finally 4) consider your marketing budget and cross off
anything that doesn't fit with your available funds. At this stage, I
would recommend that you strike any form of advertising from your
list. You will make better use of your funds by first testing the kinds
of messaging and materials your clients respond to, then investing in
advertising later, to accelerate proven campaigns.

Now look down your list and see what activities you have
underlined. Whatever you have underlined four times is the gold
standard: these are the activities that play to your strengths, fit your
Dream Clients' preferences and that you feel ready to deploy.

Choose just one activity to start with. You can always bring in
some of the other ideas later, but remember, at this stage you want
to defend your energy, to avoid becoming overwhelmed. Start with
what feels most achievable right now. And don't worry if this isn't
where you see competitors starting – remember, you are building
your business and *your* relationship with your clients. And anyway,
you can never be sure their methods work.

Starting with one activity also allows you to focus on mastering
the necessary skills, monitoring results and learning about your
clients' responses. Do your Dream Clients find your topics interesting?
Do they have additional questions? Listen closely: they are powerful
guides who can teach you the most effective way to nurture them
along their journey.

I'd encourage you to see marketing as a big experiment. Don't
demand perfection: embrace all the lessons you learn along the way
and keep testing and adapting. The key is to find an approach that
gets the desired results and feels enjoyable for you. If your chosen
strategy doesn't do both, consistency will always be a struggle.

And consistency is fundamental: it's what builds your clients' all-important know-like-trust-believe convictions towards you and your offer. If you don't enjoy creating your content, your audience won't enjoy consuming it and your results will suffer. Keep exploring and refining until you land on something you enjoy, are good at, and that genuinely serves your audience.

Repeat this same process with each subsequent step in the client journey. You might want to start with your original list each time, reviewing and expanding it to include anything additional that you have come up with along the way.

As you progress along the steps, you will increasingly want to focus on activities that engage more deeply with individuals, rather than targeting a wider group. Demonstrations, sales conversations, mini-courses, challenges and so on would only prove wasteful at the Awareness stage. But every step your prospects take along their journey demonstrates that they are responsive to some part of your messaging, and so, as they progress, you can offer more involved, personal engagement with confidence. By the time you reach the decision phase, you want to focus on engaging one-on-one, or with at most a small number of prospects at a time.

You may find that some steps feature the same activities. For example, a blog post might work equally well for those at the Awareness stage and for those at the Consideration stage. This is fine. But keep the needs of both groups in mind and ensure your content signals clearly which parts of your content answer which particular needs.

You can also link content together. For example, a blog post written for someone in the Awareness stage might link to another blog post that builds on that content for someone at the Consideration stage. This in turn might include a link to a call or sales page for those who are ready to solve their problem. It is always worthwhile to consider how each piece of content links to the next piece, and how, together, they all link to the stages of your prospects' journeys.

As you work your way through your journey map, you may notice something: the map continues beyond the sale. And so does marketing. Marketing is not just about promotion; it's about *the entire experience* you create for your clients: the people you employ; the spaces you meet with your clients (from the feng shui of your office to your choice of Zoom background); the offers you provide; the pricing you set; the processes that support your work; the look, feel and experience of your website, social media profiles, reports, presentations, brochures; the experience you create for your clients and employees.

It all has an impact on the image you project, the decisions your prospects and clients make, the results they get, and what they say about you to others. It is all part of how people experience your businesses, and so it is all part of marketing.

So continue planning your marketing through the Retention and Advocate stages of the Client Journey Map. How will you continue to surprise and delight your clients as you work together? What do you notice about how your best clients get results? Can you incentivise more clients to adopt those same behaviours and get amazing results themselves? How and when will you invite them to refer you to others? And how will you thank and reward them for doing so?

A friend once told me that your best qualification is a job. In business, the best validation of your work and impact is having clients who happily recommend you to their friends and network. But this doesn't happen by accident. Like any other relationship, it takes some work and attention. Building it into your marketing plan ensures that you follow through on your intentions and create a consistently high level of service. We will look at this process in depth in Chapter Ten.

When you have completed your updated Client Journey Map, review your chosen marketing activities in full to ensure that, when it is all taken together, everything feels doable. If the plan feels too big for you to handle on your own, either simplify your steps or look for ways you can bring in help. Then break down exactly what you need to do to make each activity happen as you'd like, and schedule these activities in your diary. Et voilà, you have your marketing plan.

Straightforward, right?

There is just one final thing to remember: when putting your marketing plan together, always keep your Value Sweet Spot paramount in your mind. It is all too easy to get carried away with what you *could* do, or what other business owners are doing. Regularly check in with your activities and content to ensure they are aligned with what *you* want to do. This is vitally important: it not only ensures you will be happy with your work and what you offer; it is essential to standing out and building a brand.

As you learn more about yourself, your value and your clients, your Value Sweet Spot may evolve. This is good. It will allow you to increase your impact over time and stay relevant for your clients. But as it does so, ensure that your Core Message, marketing plan and content evolves too.

For example, when I repositioned my business from a communication consultancy for large companies to a coaching service for small businesses, I initially started out as an advisor to female entrepreneurs. But over time, I recognised that the people who most benefitted from my approach tended to be introverted and have a specific expertise they had honed over a decade or more.

As my Value Sweet Spot has evolved to become more specific to the needs of this group, so has my messaging and marketing. It has been a subtle shift, but I've noticed that the narrower my niche grows, the more perfect my clients have become. Now the opportunities I'm presented with align beautifully with my own expertise, allowing me to have a bigger impact without having to be louder.

I've seen this same effect for my clients, affirming my conviction that success isn't about who shouts the loudest, but who resonates the deepest.

Step Buys Step

I've often seen business owners jump into marketing activities that are too advanced for their stage of business. As a result, they waste time, money and energy and ultimately delay their growth. Worse still, in some cases, they take their lack of progress as a sign that they were never meant to succeed.

There is a brilliant concept called 'Step Buys Step' that will keep you from falling into this trap. Step Buys Step is about starting small and achievable, and learning the skills, gaining the insights and earning the money needed for you to move to the next stage of growth.

It's also a great way to research your market and test what works. Here's a hypothetical example to illustrate the process:

Jane loves making cupcakes. She started out making them for her kids' parties and school events, and soon friends were asking her to make cupcakes for their own events too. She decided to start a small business from her kitchen. As word of her cupcakes grew, she looked at moving to an industrial kitchen or bakery to keep up with demand, but hesitated when she discovered the significant cost involved. So, to test if her investment would pay off, she took a smaller intermediary step and started selling cupcakes at the local food market each Saturday.

Her market stand helped her test which sizes, flavours, textures and decorations sold best to the general public. She got to speak to her clients directly, and she learned more about their needs, ideas, and how they described her cakes and their place in their lives. This gave her words and insights she could build into her marketing, to help it resonate instantly with her Dream Clients. She also started to build brand recognition, leading to repeat customers and more orders.

This gave her the information, money, client base and confidence she needed for the next stage. She started by renting a bigger kitchen and employed a friend to help her with the production, distribution and sales. She was then able to venture into catering and selling to other businesses. Again, she listened, learned and noted the feedback of these clients. Soon she had what she needed for the next step: her own store.

And so the journey continued. At each stage, not only was Jane earning money, developing the skills and confidence she needed to excel, and learning about her market, she was discovering how to propel herself into the next stage of business growth. Step Buys Step gave her everything she needed to keep growing and succeeding without feeling overwhelmed by her decisions, investments or the steep learning curve.

Had she gone straight from her home kitchen to a store, she wouldn't have had the skills, understanding, brand recognition, mindset, customers or funding for a smooth and easy transition. Learning and building everything she needed to make a success of a store could well have taken longer than her modest budget would have lasted. Not only that, but it might have been such a stressful process that she would have completely burned out.

Remember the stairs analogy from earlier? This doesn't just apply to the client journey. Often the fastest, most comfortable and robust way to achieve your vision is to slow down and go one step at a time. In other words, as you build your marketing plan, dream big but plan small.

What to Do If You Feel Stuck or Marketing Feels Hard

If a particular marketing activity feels hard, take a step back and try to identify what's causing the difficulty. I typically find that it's one of four reasons.

1) It's pushing your comfort zone

Pushing yourself will always feel uncomfortable, but sometimes we have to embrace discomfort. Remember what all this effort is for: it will lead you to important personal growth, and take you and your business to the next level.

Consider reaching out to someone in your network who can help you through the struggle. For example, when AI came on the scene, I didn't know where to start, so I ignored it. Then I met AI wizard Nino Giambalvo, who helped me create my first custom ChatGPT assistant. Since then, I've been hooked and have been happily experimenting and growing ever since.

2) You have a skills gap

In this case you have a choice: learn the skill or outsource the activity. To decide which path to take, consider how powerful a particular skill is for your business, and how often it will be needed. For example, when I was starting out, I knew my business would need a lot of sales pages, so I dedicated myself to mastering the process of creating one.

It doesn't mean you'll be stuck performing this skill forever. I have since outsourced this task, and my knowledge of the discipline helped me find and train the right person to delegate it to.

3) You have too many things going on

Reassess your priorities and see what you can stop or put on hold. I find myself butting up against this issue a lot! I'm a master at generating new ideas, and I have to remind myself to periodically assess their importance, so that I avoid feeling overwhelmed.

4) Fear

When it comes to marketing, it's common to experience some fear, particularly the fear of judgement. It's easy to question whether people won't like or will disagree with our content. What will our friends think of us? Who are we to say this anyway?'

The list goes on. We'll cover mindset in Part Three. But for now, simply remind yourself of your dream clients – how they are struggling today, and how your content can help them. If people think negative things, it's only because your content wasn't intended for them.

Create an Inspiration Bank

I'd like to encourage you to listen, watch and read widely. Inspiration for your marketing and content is all around you. Follow other people and think about why you like or dislike their work, and what you can learn from it to apply to your own content.

Create a document or folder where you can keep your ideas safe. Keep notes of phrases, content, images, activities, etc. that stand out to you, and note down why. The idea isn't to copy someone else's words and ideas; not only is this unethical, but it won't help you stand out for your own values and ideas. The idea is to stay open to learning.

Accelerating Your Growth

Once you know what works in your marketing, the next step is to amplify those efforts so you can grow your business more quickly and with greater ease. Growing your business is not just about more profit, though that is of course important. It's about becoming sustainable, having more impact for your clients and industry, and creating more opportunities for others.

You have already built the foundations; now it's time to lean into strategies that expand your reach and connect you with more of your Dream Clients.

Here are some simple yet powerful ways to accelerate your growth:

- **Get in front of other people's audiences.** Podcasts, group trainings, summits and events give you access to communities your Dream Clients already belong to. Appearing on such platforms lets you borrow the trust the host has built, boosting your visibility and credibility, and can grow your audience quickly. Be bold and reach out to big players as well as those who feel more accessible. One 'Yes!' from an established thought leader could mean a big leap in your business growth. Focus on adding value to the audience and showing gratitude to the host, who may have spent years curating her group. Do this and you may be invited back again.

- **Collaborate with complementary businesses.** Partner with others who share your values and serve your audience but in complementary ways. For example, a web designer might team up with a copywriter or brand photographer. Joint workshops, referral partnerships, giveaways and events, or bundled services create more value for your clients, while multiplying your reach. Collaborating with others can also increase your knowledge and confidence, as well as being fun.

- **Experiment with advertising.** Once your messaging and offers are tested, ads can be a powerful way to get in front of more of the right people. Start small, track results, and scale only what works. If you are new to advertising, expect a learning curve. It often takes a few months for ads to become a predictable source of leads.

- **Encourage referrals and introductions.** We have discussed how happy clients love to spread the word about your services, especially if you make it easy. Provide them with a simple blurb or example of who to refer so they know exactly how to help.

- **Reuse and repurpose your best content.** Don't reinvent the wheel. Use great content more than once and aim to repurpose it in many ways to expand your reach. A post that resonates on LinkedIn, for example, can become an email, adapted for other social media platforms, turned into a video, expanded into a podcast or even a guest article. Repurposing saves time while multiplying your impact.

- **Showcase case studies and success stories.** Sharing real examples of the difference you've made builds instant credibility and inspires confidence. Stories often travel further than statistics, and they are certainly more memorable and engaging. They also illustrate your WAW Factor in practice, adding another layer of belief in your ability to deliver your promise.

Each of these strategies helps you reach more of the right people faster, without adding unnecessary complexity or draining your energy. Remember, the goal isn't to do everything, but to double down on what already works and then amplify it in a way that feels aligned with you and your Dream Clients.

CHAPTER SUMMARY

- Focus on marketing activities that suit your current skills, values, personality and strengths, so they feel comfortable and enjoyable, allowing you to be consistent.

- Never compare yourself to others or copy their ideas. Everyone has their own Value Sweet Spot and objectives, so comparing yourself will only result in self-doubt and dilution. Instead, be inspired and keep learning, improving and growing.

- Map your marketing to your client journey. This ensures that all your messaging has a clear purpose and supports your prospects in taking sure, steady steps towards becoming paying clients.

- Always invite your audience to take the next step in their journey.

- Using a Step-Buys-Step approach helps build the skills, confidence, clients and resources needed for your next level of growth. These smaller steps often result in faster and longer-lasting growth overall.

- If something in your marketing plan feels hard to implement, or you catch yourself procrastinating, take a step back, assess what might be the cause and decide your best steps forward.

- As you learn what works well, accelerate your growth by getting in front of other people's audiences, partnering with other business owners and thought leaders, asking for referrals, experimenting with advertising, sharing case studies and making more of your most successful content.

Sidenote: There are so many different ways you can market your business that it would have been impossible to list them here without distracting from the main content! I have created a separate document for you in the resources that accompany this book, listing the most common marketing methods and my tips on making these work. This includes everything from social media, email and websites to PR, podcasts and flyers. You can download it and other resources at: www.melittacampbell.com/ValueWhisperingBook

Chapter Eight

Successful Sales Conversations

Your sales conversations can be highly valuable experiences that serve your client deeply and help them enjoy better outcomes.

In my first business, my communication consultancy, I never had sales conversations. Or at least that's what I thought. A client would contact me, I'd ask questions to identify their problem and see how I could help them; then I'd send them a proposal, often enough they'd say 'Yes!', and we'd start working together.

At that time, I thought sales conversations were all about hard selling, clever talking and convincing people to buy whether they were ready to or not. I now know better. Sales done well is not at all like that. It's about asking good questions, listening closely, and helping your prospect understand their own needs and how they want to solve their problem. Then it's about exploring possible solutions. In other words, it's about caring, guiding and holding space. Exactly what I'd been doing all along.

And you probably have been too. If you are an introvert and you've been telling yourself that you are no good at sales, I want you to think again. Your natural tendency to ask meaningful questions, actively listen, think deeply and understand fully before making a proposition is *exactly* what valuable sales conversations are based on.

Add a simple structure to that conversation, and you'll be well on your way to having successful and enjoyable sales conversations — ones that you and your prospect find enjoyable and valuable.

And here's more good news: you already have most of what you need for this structure: a distinct niche, a great offer and a clear message. Better still...

If you have followed the earlier processes in this book, mapping your marketing to the client journey and aligning your activities to your Value Sweet Spot, when your dream prospect books a sales call with you, they will already know, like and trust you, *and* they will already believe you have the solution and ability to help them. They'll just have a few questions to ensure that your offer really is the best next step for them.

This is where structuring your conversation can help. This structure has nothing to do with pushy sales tactics; it's just a simple process to ensure you can help your prospect uncover all their most pressing needs, answer all their questions and respond to any concerns, before inviting them to learn more about your offer. I like to think of this conversation as your opportunity to become your prospect's champion and guide.

And remember, your sales conversation is your chance to audition your prospect as much as it's theirs to audition you. You don't want to work with just any clients; you only want to work with your Dream Clients. Those are the people who will help you to grow and scale your business, and for whom you can create a meaningful impact. So weave in questions that will tell you more about their values, intentions and readiness to commit to their own success.

If during your conversation you discover that your offer isn't right for your prospect, that's OK. Be honest about this and don't try and sell to them. This will build trust and credibility and may, on occasion, even result in them referring business to you.

This has happened to me several times. For example, when I was running my communication consultancy, I had one prospect who it became apparent wasn't right for my services. I told her this and explained why, and as our call had helped her to understand my offer and skills, over the next five years she referred four high-ticket clients to me. And when her own circumstances changed and she returned for another conversation, we agreed that this *was* the perfect project for us to collaborate on, and she became a client herself.

The Anatomy of a Successful Sales Conversation

Now you understand that sales conversations are not about being pushy, you may already feel more at ease with the idea of your next one. But if you're anything like me, positive vibes won't be enough. You'll want to know exactly what to ask and exactly when to ask it. You'll want to be sure that both you and your prospect have got all the information needed to make the right decision. That's why a clear structure matters. It also helps you to feel calm and confident in the moment, so you can focus on your prospect and their responses.

I like to think of my sales conversations in six parts.

1. Building rapport. You need your prospect to share their situation, challenges and dreams with you openly and honestly. This requires trust. While you may have built this before the call, you still need to consolidate a strong connection early in your conversation. It's a small step, but it will make all the difference to your success. With AI-generated content becoming so common, this is your chance to show your authenticity.

Start with one or two easy to answer questions that show you are interested in them as a person, not just as a potential sale. Here are some examples:

'What's great with you today?'

'Where are you calling in from?'

'It looks sunny where you are. Is that typical at this time of year?'

'I love that ornament/painting/book title. Is there a story behind that?'

2. Understanding your prospect. While building rapport might only take a few minutes, you want to take your time with this next part. You want to know and understand as much relevant information about your prospect as possible. When you are clear about where they are today, why they feel stuck, what success for them looks like, and why it matters, you'll be in a strong position to know if your offer is right for them, and what aspects of your offer will appeal to them most. Make good notes as you go, because what you learn in this part of your conversation will help you with the sale and any subsequent follow up.

Questions to ask:

'I'd love to learn more about you, where you're at right now and where you're trying to get to. Could you tell me more about [your topic]?' Follow this up with clarifying questions such as: 'Why do you want that?' 'What's stopping you from having that today?' 'What would it mean for you if you got that?' 'Is that important to you? Why?' 'How will you know if you have it?'

'If everything went perfectly, where would you like to be in the next six-to-twelve months from now? How will that feel? What will that do for you? Why is that important?'

'What do you think has been holding you back or standing in your way?'

'Is there anything else that would hold you back from the results you would like?'

'Why does now feel like the right time for you to solve this?'

'If you had the right support and framework, do you feel you have the time and commitment to work towards your desired outcomes right now?'

Keep going with your questions until you feel you've uncovered their three biggest problems or reasons to work with you. As you plan your sales call structure, it may feel like you have a lot of questions to ask. However, in practice, these questions help with the conversation flow and, if you are giving your prospect the space to answer each question fully, they will feel caring and valuable as you give your prospect ample opportunity to explore their challenge and situation and gain real clarity.

3. The check-in. Now you want to verify you've understood everything correctly. A quick check-in will help confirm you are both on the same page, clarify any misconceptions, and sometimes might reveal an even bigger problem or motivation that has been missed.

Question to ask:

'So, you are currently [here] and you want to be [here]. And when you get there, it will allow you to [this] so you can enjoy more of [this] – did I understand that correctly?'

4. The sale. If you believe that your offer can help your prospect solve their problem in a way that is both meaningful for them and aligns with your values and situation, then you want to invite them to learn more about it.

This is the part many business owners find challenging. But remember, if you don't tell them how you can help, then they will just keep on struggling. Worse still, they may go to someone else who doesn't have such a strong proposition as you! Inviting them to solve their problem with you is not simply self-interest; it's putting yourself forward to be of service. Here are some ways you could invite them to learn more about your offer. Customise these in whatever ways feel right for you.

Questions to ask:

'I believe my [service/programme] can help you get the results you've mentioned today. Would you like me to tell you how it works?'

'From what you've told me, I believe I can help you with [your problem] through my [service/programme]. Would you like to discuss what it would look like for us to work together?'

'If we could work together towards the results you've just told me about, would that be interesting for you?'

Did you notice how these questions didn't ask your prospect if they want to buy? Never sell to someone without their permission. Ask the question, and if you have done the first three parts well, your prospect will be excited to hear about how you can help.

The biggest mistake business owners make at this point is racing through their offer. If someone is going to invest time and money in your solution, they will want to understand it fully, so take your time to explain everything about your offer as completely as you can. As you do, regularly pause and check in with your prospect by asking: 'Does that make sense?' That will give them the opportunity to ask questions, gain further clarification if needed, and feel part of the discussion. Remember not to focus too much on the features, but instead to highlight all your offer's WAW Factors.

Sarah's Story

When Sarah first came to me, she had a regular stream of prospects, but because of her low closure rate and frequent discounting, she dreaded every call.

When we discussed her sales call process, she realised that, when she shared her skills, experience and services with her clients, her value wasn't coming across clearly. As a result, clients would only buy into a small part of her service and/or push down her prices.

I see many business owners making this same mistake. They talk about their certifications, tools and other features, assuming their prospect will understand how these translate into value. But this is rarely the case. You need to share your Signature System, and relate your WAW Factor to the needs of your clients. *That* is how you make it clear what you can do for them.

Remember, you are the expert in how to solve your client's problem. So it's up to you to tell your prospect what you believe is best for them. Don't leave it up to them to try and figure this out. Most won't.

Once Sarah understood her Value Sweet Spot, she saw that she had so much more to offer than she was presenting to her clients. By creating a Signature System, she was able to simply and clearly explain her True Value and how their businesses and profits would transform after working with her. And by having a clear structure for her sales calls, she could confidently lead the conversation to this critical point.

As a result, her sales calls became easy and enjoyable for both her and her prospects, and she was able to sell bigger packages and stop offering discounts.

Within weeks she was able to confidently increase her prices, had begun to work with better quality clients, and been able to start paying herself and her team accordingly.

5. Saying your price. Once you have explained your offer, there is just one thing left to tell your prospect: the price!

If inviting a prospect to learn more about your offer is hard, telling them the price can feel even harder. As a result, many business owners will be ready to offer a discount and all sorts of extras before the prospect has even had a chance to respond. Resist this temptation.

Low pricing and discounts are rarely good strategies for small businesses. They erode your profit and leave you feeling like you aren't valued, negatively impacting your ability to show up and do your best work.

And if you are not profitable, you won't be able to help your clients over the long term, or have the impact in the world you set out to create. So price fairly. That means that your price accurately reflects the value your client receives and your skill, expertise and commitment. In other words, it's fair to them and fair to you.

Share this fair price with your prospect and then stay quiet. You want to give them space to think through all the information you've provided and decide for themselves if they see value in your offer. I once had a prospect who was silent for ten minutes. It took a lot of effort to stay quiet myself, I can tell you! But when she did finally speak, it was a 'Yes', and she thanked me for giving her the space to consider everything without feeling under pressure to respond. If I'd spoken too soon, I might not have got the sale, and she wouldn't have got the help she needed.

Often, your prospect won't be aware of the typical price of an offer like yours. Therefore, it can be helpful to weave a price comparison early on in your discussion, before you mention your actual price, to help frame your pricing and ensure your offer stands out as great value.

6. The decision. Waiting for a prospect's answer can be nerve-wracking, but remember, if they are taking their time, it means they must be seriously considering everything you've shared. So keep breathing and smiling as you wait.

If they say no, thank them for their time, and feel free to ask them for some clarification. 'If you wouldn't mind telling me, what would have made this a yes for you?' Knowing more might help you better position your offer in the future.

Also, keep in mind that a 'No' now, doesn't always mean a 'No' forever. Their situation can change at any time, and they may simply have booked a call with you too early in their client journey. Therefore, be sure to follow up with those who don't buy right away. You can add them to your email list, so they hear from your regularly, and you may want to reach out with a specific call or message every few months.

You can also ask your noes for a referral. 'I understand that this isn't right for you at this time, but now you know more about how I help [your clients], are you aware of anyone else looking to [achieve these goals] who might value my support in doing so?'

It doesn't always get a referral, but it's always worth asking.

If they say yes, celebrate with them and show your excitement. Explain what will happen next and give them their first action to take. For example, in my signature programme, the Value Whispering™ Blueprint programme, I have a module with mini-tasks for my new clients to complete. Each task helps them to set out their intentions and plans, encouraging them to feel excited about the results they are to begin working towards.

Some of my clients offer their clients something to read, or an exercise to complete before their first session together. Immediately giving your new client something worthwhile to do can prevent them from experiencing 'buyer's remorse' — that sinking moment of doubt we all have when we've invested in something big and have yet to experience its value.

If they want to think about it. It's not uncommon for people to want some time before making a decision, either to think things through or to discuss it with someone else. Sure, in some cases, this is a tactic to avoid having to tell you 'No'. But in most cases, it's genuine.

You can never be quite sure what they are really thinking, but you can ask some questions to ensure they feel supported as they reflect on your offer. For example, you can ask what they feel they need to reflect on. This question may reveal some questions that you haven't yet answered.

I would also recommend that you book a short follow-up call with your prospect before you end your current call. This will prevent a lengthy game of email ping pong and reduce the risk of being ghosted. Between calls, send them a summary of your offer and anything else that is relevant, such as case studies or articles that show how you have helped solve their problem for other clients.

Handling Objections

When people push back, it can feel like we are being rejected as people, and this can cause us to get defensive. At such moments, it's important to remember that questions and challenges are good. They indicate that your prospect is trying to see how your offer might work for them in practice. They are engaging with what you have to say, so I encourage you to take a deep breath, smile and get curious.

Listen carefully to their thoughts and questions and seek to understand why these are important to them. The reasons behind their objections aren't always what you might expect. By staying open and holding the space for your prospect, you can often turn objections in your favour.

Before your call, it is worthwhile anticipating common objections and preparing clear responses and follow up questions. The key is to focus on understanding and addressing their underlying concerns. The following questions will help:

'That's interesting, why do you ask that?'

'Great question, can you tell me more?'

'Is that something that's particularly important to you? Why?'

'Is that a game-changer for you?'

Listen out for key words in their objection and repeat them. For example, if they were to say, 'I'm not sure I have the time for this,' you can reply, 'The time?' This will usually prompt them to expand on their point and tell you what is on their mind. You can then guide them appropriately.

To avoid objections at the end of your call, you can proactively seek them out earlier in your discussion, by asking questions like:

'What are your thoughts so far?'

'What concerns do you have?'

'Is there any reason why we shouldn't move forward?'

'Have you considered your budget?'

'What might get in the way of you making a decision today?'

Bringing It All Together

To help you have consistently great sales conversations, create a simple sales script. This should lay out the questions you want to ask, in order, and specify every point to make when you explain your offer in detail

A clear, simple structure has many benefits. It means you can focus on your prospects' words, rather than thinking about what to ask next. And it will ensure you cover everything you need to comprehensively guide your prospect to the right decision for them. Plus, having a logical, measured flow to your pitch will give your client confidence in your abilities as a service-provider.

Following this structure will also help you avoid oversharing. Sometimes we can give too much information away, information that misleads your prospect into feeling they now understand how to move forward without any further help from you. This perception will almost always do them a disservice; unless your service boils down to one core piece of advice, it's unlikely their problem can be resolved so easily.

Once you have your draft script, check that it aligns with your Value Sweet Spot. To do this, ask yourself these two questions:

If you were to conduct the *perfect* sales conversation, one where you and your prospect were in total alignment with what was important and valuable, and where you both agreed completely on the nature of their problem, how would you feel during and after your call?

Does anything in your script need to change to help that happen?

Review and refine your call structure often, to ensure it incorporates everything you learn from your calls. Over time, this will help you make it more natural and impactful.

Building Your Sales Confidence

It's important that you go into every sales call with the right mindset. If you don't believe in your offer or doubt your ability to help your Dream Clients get the results they seek, then your prospect won't believe in these either.

Answer the following questions to help you build a rock-solid belief in your work and the results you create:

'What is your Dream Client struggling with today and how does your product or service help with this?'

'What will their life be like after they work with you?'

'Why is helping your client get results important to you?'

'What do you love/hate to happen for your clients?'

'How have other people benefited from working with you in the past?'

'How do you feel about these transformations and outcomes?'

Review your answers and highlight those points you have the strongest belief in or emotional connection with. Turn these into affirmations that you can repeat to yourself before every sales call: for example, 'I guide my clients to life-changing transformations.'

Before your sales calls, take some time to centre yourself. Then read these affirmations along with some of your client testimonials to help yourself feel confident and ready for a great conversation.

Once your client says, 'Heck yes!' to working with you, you can guide them to the next step in the client journey: Onboarding.

CHAPTER SUMMARY

- Successful sales conversations require you to build rapport and help your client understand their problem and how they would like to solve it. This requires you to ask great questions, actively listen, reflect and guide your prospect through your conversation – all skills that come naturally to most introverts.

- If you have followed the processes in this book, your prospect will come to your sales call already knowing, liking and trusting you, and believing you could be their perfect service-provider.

- Having a simple sales call structure will help you ask the right questions at the right time, and allow you to refine these questions over time.

- Value Whispering™ sales conversations have six parts: building rapport, understanding your prospect, the check-in, the price, the sale, the decision.

- Objections and questions are good. They show that your prospect is actively trying to fit your solution into their life and situation. They give you and your prospect an opportunity to gain even deeper insights and clarity around the best solution for your prospect.

- A simple one-page document that reminds you of the value you create for your clients can help you go into every sales conversation with confidence.

Chapter Nine

Onboarding and Nurturing Your Clients

Onboarding isn't just about admin. It's about kickstarting your relationship with your new client, and setting the tone for their success story.

Congratulations! You have a wonderful new client. This is the moment your relationship takes on a new dimension and you can significantly step up the value you create.

It's exciting! But like all things, a little planning and process can go a long way to increasing your impact while also lowering the time required to set up your new client for success.

Having a pre-designed process for onboarding and nurturing clients will help you add more value, accelerate client results and support your ongoing business growth.

Look back to your Client Journey Map to remind yourself of how you want your client to feel as they take their first steps as your newest client and, in particular, how you can operate within your Value Sweet Spot to begin making a magical difference in their lives.

Then ask the following questions:

1. 'How do I believe people get the best results from working with me?'

2. 'What do my best clients do differently that help them get great results?'

3. 'What makes my clients feel confident and ready for action?'

Free write your answers and keep adding ideas until nothing more comes to mind. You'll already have some of the answers from the work you did earlier in the Value Whispering™ process. Write them down with your new ideas so all your material is in one place.

Now look through your work and start to identify ways you can build these insights into onboarding and client care processes. Get creative and don't dismiss any ideas just yet. I've often seen wacky ideas develop into exciting new ways to create value. Mix impractical thoughts with more achievable ideas, and you might just create something special.

For example. when I was head of communication for the international private banking arm of Lloyds Bank, based in Geneva, I was part of a team tasked with rebranding the business. We allowed ourselves to go crazy, throwing around any ideas that came into our head. 'Add sparkles!' came one suggestion. We all laughed and kept on suggesting new concepts.

But when we researched card stock for the brochures and business cards, we found one that really stood out: a luxurious card – with sparkles! Our clients loved the result, and our team won a 'Making a Difference' award, one of only twenty-eight given across

28,000 staff at the bank. Don't underestimate where your crazy ideas may take you.

In fact, let's add that as a bonus question:

4. 'What wild and crazy things would surprise, delight and add incredible value for your clients?'

Once you have all your ideas, it's time to turn them into a plan. What will help your new client feel comfortable, valued and ready for action from day one? Look back through your answers and highlight your strongest responses. Then start to organise your list according to what you can already do, and what might take more time and thought to create. Then plan out your actions and get started. Easy as that!

As you create your plan, try and favour those activities that can be automated or created in advance. This will help you deliver a consistently high standard as your business grows.

Finally, take care not to overwhelm your new client with too many things to do. Review your plan from their perspective and see if any of your brilliant ideas can be simplified or perhaps integrated later.

For my Value Whispering™ Blueprint clients, I have created a sequence of automated emails that are triggered as soon as someone joins the programme. In the first two weeks, they receive several short messages to help them get oriented. The sequence continues over the lifespan of the programme, giving additional tips, guiding them to some of the more advanced materials, and checking in with their progress. My clients often remark how much they appreciate these emails – how they make them feel seen and valued, even though they are aware that the messages are automated.

I also created a special module in the online training platform that accompanies the programme, again to help clients quickly orient themselves. After the first year of the programme, I noticed that those clients who had a clear goal for the programme tended to put more in and get more out. So I expanded this initial module with short videos and simple workbooks that guided new clients to create their vision and formulate their intentions and goals, so more of my clients could deepen their results.

Once you put your onboarding process into action, regularly review it against what your most successful clients are doing, to see if there are any refinements you can make.

Ongoing Client Care

The form of much of your ongoing client care will come directly from the work you do with your client: how you help your clients accomplish their goals is how you care for them. But you can continue to whisper your value and nurture your client relationship with an intentional client care process.

This can include regular (possibly automated) check-in emails and/or surveys. These can help you monitor progress and spot areas for improvement. Bonus or surprise events can help you to deepen your value and keep your client relationships fresh and active, and cards and small gifts can be simple ways to help your clients feel appreciated.

You may feel that automation lacks the human touch, but it's better to be consistent than to have one client receive amazing care while another falls through the cracks. If you are strongly opposed to pre-written automated emails, then simply create a series of templates accompanied by a system that gives you a nudge when it's time to send a particular email, so you can personalise the message before hitting 'Send'.

Asking for Testimonials, Reviews and Referrals

In chapter six, I discuss the value of social proof — testimonials that your services work. People prefer to do what they see other people like them doing, so you want to request reviews and testimonials on a regular basis, and to build these requests into your client care system.

The timing of your review requests will depend on your type of offer. For a power-hour session, you'll want to ask straight away. For a longer programme, it usually makes sense to wait a while. That said, don't wait until the end of a client relationship, because you may find you have to chase your client, and often it feels awkward to keep asking. It can be more powerful to request a testimonial sooner — not only because their experience will still be fresh in their mind, but because they know they will see you again. It encourages the sense of accountability that will get them to actively write and share their review. And if you time your request for directly after they've thanked you or had a big win, that's perfect.

There are several ways clients can provide reviews or testimonials. The first is to write one and email it to you. However, I prefer to ask them to provide a recommendation on LinkedIn or Google, so it's immediately publicly available and clear they have written it themselves. I can then share their review on my website or other marketing materials.

Consider which platforms will provide the most value and actively ask for your clients to review you there. If you are asking for reviews on multiple platforms, think about ways you can make this an easy process. Clarity, ease and convenience are the biggest drivers of action. For example, you could email a client a copy of a recommendation they left on LinkedIn, tell them how much you appreciate it, and then, providing the direct link to the right page, ask if they would be happy to share it as a Google review.

For my business, I've decided to split my reviews. I ask clients of my private coaching or Value WhisperingTM Blueprint programme to share their reviews on LinkedIn, as these are usually longer. Then I ask people who have booked a shorter session or attended one of my free events for a short Google review. The contrast of longer testimonials and shorter reviews gives me a lot of flexibility when it comes to using these assets in my marketing materials.

Most clients will be happy to provide a review and support your business, but sometimes they aren't sure what to say. They'll often appreciate some support (remember, convenience and ease drive action). There are two ways I like to do this. The first is to provide them with a suggested structure to follow, based on three to five questions. For example:

'Why did you decide to work with me?'

'Where is your business now, versus where it was when we first started working together?'

'What have you appreciated most?'

'Who else do you feel would benefit from this programme?'

A structure like this not only makes it easier for your client, but also helps them answer precisely the questions future Dream Clients will have about working with you.

Alternatively, write the review for them based on something they have already told you. Then send it across as a suggestion and invite them to add/delete/change as they see fit. If you have regular check-in surveys or emails with your clients, you may find they've already written a perfect review. Send it to them along with some appreciation and a simple request to use it within your messaging.

Referrals are a little different. These are personal recommendations your clients (or partners) make directly to a specific person or audience. They are extremely powerful. Again, it can be helpful to build requests for referrals into your client care system, to ensure a regular supply.

You might like to build an incentive scheme around your referrals, but if you do, ensure that any referrals are likely to align with your Value Sweet Spot and that the incentive itself is appropriate in size and value.

As with reviews, a great time to ask for referrals is after a client has thanked you. You can reply with a simple request: 'I'm so pleased you are finding our time together valuable. In fact, I would love to help more people like you to get amazing results like these. Is there someone in your network who you feel might benefit from this programme/service?' If you can replace the 'someone' in that sentence with a short description of your Dream Client, all the better.

I know from my own experience that asking for reviews and referrals can feel awkward. But I want you to remember that your goal is to help others. And there *are* people out there who are actively looking for your help. You owe it to them to make the request. And trust me, once you've asked a couple of times, and had a positive response, then you'll soon feel more comfortable.

On that point, if you are finding this book helpful, then I would appreciate it if you could take a moment to leave a review on Amazon or Good Reads. There are more people like you struggling to create marketing plans that feel aligned to their vision, value and personality. Your review will help them find this book, and lead them to the Value Whispering™ Blueprint, saving them from hours of frustration. Oh, and if you send me a snapshot of your review, or tag me in a social media post that mentions the book, I will send you a special bonus to say thank you.

See? It's as easy as that!

CHAPTER SUMMARY

- When it comes to onboarding your new clients and nurturing them through your service, a little planning and automation can create a valuable and enjoyable experience and help them enjoy smoother results faster.

- Consider what you can do to help your clients quickly feel confident and ready for action. Look at what your most successful clients do for ideas.

- Sometimes your craziest ideas can lead to exciting new ways to delight your clients and stand out in your marketplace.

- Regularly review your onboarding and nurturing processes to see what can be simplified, improved or automated.

- It's important to build asking for referrals, reviews and testimonials into the way you run your business. These provide future clients with the social proof that your service works for people like them.

- Consider which platforms make the most sense for which kind of review, so you can guide your clients to the right place.

- Consider how you can make providing testimonials and reviews easy.

Part Three

Self-Leadership

There is a lot we can do to manage our energy, time, focus and mindset. When we set boundaries around what works for us, there is no limit to the positive impact we can create for ourselves and others.

The most popular episodes of my podcast, *The Art of Value Whispering*, are those that discuss getting things done. Like episode 246: 'I know what to do, so why aren't I doing it?!'

Unfortunately, there is no single answer to this question. Our ability to get things done on any given day depends on many factors: from how energised we are, to how confident and capable we feel about a particular task, to the situations or rooms we find ourselves in. And these factors can change daily.

But there is hope! While there may not be a magic bullet to solve the problem of personal productivity, there are still many things we can control.

In this chapter, I will break down some of the most common reasons why we, as business owners and introverts, feel slowed down or held back, and what we can do to create the conditions to flow smoothly towards our goals.

There is a lot we can do to manage our energy, time, focus and mindset, and I'm excited to share what I've seen work best.

This chapter comes with a caveat, however. What works for you may be different to what works for other people. We all have different personalities, visions, preferences, ways of thinking and operating, skills and experiences. Likewise, we are all in different seasons of life and business. When I started my first business, I was thirty-three and bouncing a five-month-old baby next to my desk. Today, I'm fifty-one and navigating teenagers, perimenopause, and an unruly garden! Across the intervening years, what has helped me to stay on track and function at my most creative and productive has changed. You may experience the same thing, and find it helpful to return to this chapter as you and your business evolve.

But whichever strategies, tools and tactics you choose for yourself, do so in the knowledge that if it works for you, it works. Period.

Chapter Ten

Finding the Time and Energy for Growth

Focus and productivity are personal.
If it works for you, it works.

One of the biggest issues business owners face isn't necessarily their marketing, but finding the time and energy to put their plans into action consistently. Growing your business is a marathon, and like any marathon it can feel draining. But if you stop, your business growth stops too. Techniques to overcome challenges of energy and motivation are some of the most fundamental business skills you can learn.

Your One Page Achievement Planner

I used to have a To Do list that felt ten feet long – and growing all the time. At the end of every day, I'd look down at my list and feel so disappointed with my progress. No matter what items I'd checked off, I was only reminded of how much I had left to do.

Then I stumbled across the idea of a grid system. Without any exaggeration, this one simple technique changed my life, both professional and personal, helping me to remain focused on what's most important, so I feel accomplished at the end of the day.

Here's how to try it out for yourself. Get an A4 page and create a 2x2 grid in the middle. Then title and fill the boxes as follows:

Top-left square: Focus

In this square, write one-to-three things you need to focus on today. If you like, next to each task, also write the time you expect it to take. This helps you check that you haven't put down more things than you can realistically complete.

Bottom-left square: Next

In this square, list what you plan to work on next. Now you not only know what to move on to if you finish your 'Focus' tasks, but better yet, you have a clear dividing line between priority tasks and secondary tasks. So don't just dive into the next set of tasks without thinking. Consider if doing something else might serve you better, like taking a walk, doing some stretches, or reading a book.

Top-right square: Projects

In this square, write the bigger initiatives you are working on this quarter. Ideally, there will be no more than three of these, but depending on their size and complexity, you could include up to five. By noting your projects, you can keep the bigger picture in mind. If a new opportunity comes up, compare it against your existing projects and consider if it is more important. If you conclude that it is, choose one of your items to put off until next quarter, to make room for the new project.

Bottom-right square: Manage

In this square, list all the other things in your business or life that you need to keep an eye on, but are not directly responsible for. This could be projects your team are working on, a test your child has coming up, travel or engagements your partner is involved in – anything you need to keep in mind.

This grid gives you a snapshot of where you are and what you need to do next. But at the same time, it keeps your To Do items from feeling overwhelming. At the end of every day, you'll feel accomplished, since you've marked off your most important tasks.

I've also expanded my grid to include a series of additional boxes: my biggest goal; how I want to show up for myself and my clients; how I want to take care of my wellbeing, mindset and growth; and how I can appreciate the good in each day. I've included a copy of this full achievement planner in the resources that accompany this book at: www.melittacampbell.com/valuewhisperingbook

Tasks Versus Projects

The single biggest mistake I see my clients make – one so disastrous it can destroy their productivity and leave them disappointed and overwhelmed – is mixing up projects and tasks. At first glance, this might not seem catastrophic. But knowing the difference is at the foundation of getting things done in a manageable way.

Making these distinctions sometimes takes a bit of thought. A quick rule of thumb is that, if you can break something into distinct sections, it's a project.

Think of it this way: you probably haven't read this book in a single sitting. (And if you have, I hope you've been doing all the exercises as you go!) Each time you sit down to read, you probably have some kind of goal in mind for that session – for example to read up to, then complete, the next exercise. A few sessions later, and here you are, with the book almost finished. A series of *tasks* – completing the next exercise – has added up to a completed *project* – reading the book.

All too often I see people listing projects on their To Do list instead of individual tasks. Doing this, you risk two things: 1) the 'task' feels so big it can be hard to know where to start, and procrastination kicks in; and 2) your 'task' takes much longer than anticipated. This can throw off your other 'tasks' and leave you questioning your abilities.

Here are some common projects I see posing as tasks: 'create my website', 'publish a blog post', 'pitch to podcasts', 'develop a lead magnet', 'send a newsletter', 'launch an online course', 'create a webinar'.

None of these are tasks. In fact, many are quite large projects involving multiple stages, decisions and actions. Without breaking these down into individual steps, then prioritising and scheduling them, little gets done (except maybe some household chores or brewing multiple cups of coffee).

Here are three signs that you have a project on your hands, rather than a task:

- You feel unsure where to start. This is a sign that there are multiple steps involved.

- It will take you more than an hour to complete. This is a sign that you need to break your 'task' into more than one step.

- Parts of your task could be delegated – another sign that there are multiple steps involved.

Double check your To Do list for any projects that can be broken down into multiple tasks.

Your Don't Dos

I once heard a story about Warren Buffet and his driver. When Warren asked his driver what he'd like to accomplish before retiring, the driver responded with a long list of ambitions. Warren encouraged him to take some time to reflect and choose *one* goal to focus on first.

When the driver returned with his top priority, Warren asked, 'What will you do about the other goals on your list?' The driver admitted he'd probably try to fit them in between working on his main goal. Warren pointed out that, if he did that, he'd never achieve his priority. Instead, he advised putting those other goals on a 'Do Not Do at Any Cost' list, so he could focus fully on what mattered most. Only after accomplishing his number one priority should he return to the list and choose the next objective to pursue.

I'm not sure if this story is true, but the lesson still holds. When we try to do too much at once, we risk failing to complete anything. I'd encourage you to stick strictly to those priorities you have set in your achievement planner. When I find myself with too many goals, I like to remind myself of some wise advice a mentor once shared: 'You can't ride two horses with one arse!'

That said, there are always a small number of core activities that we need to do each day to ensure our business runs smoothly and continues to grow. These are items we never really check off a list. They're closer to tasks like eating breakfast: we need to do them as a matter of routine.

Take some time to identify these, and dedicate the first hour of each day to completing them before turning your focus to what you have written in your planner's Priority box.

It can help to have some accountability around your most important tasks. A coach once told me that we do two things in life: what we love, and what we are being watched on. When you are your own boss or work alone, it's easy to focus on all those tasks you enjoy and to neglect the more challenging responsibilities, no matter how important they might be.

There are many sources of accountability. You can hire a coach or mentor, join a mastermind or business group, ask a friend or colleague to act as your accountability buddy, track your progress in a visible way, work in a public space or publicly share your goals and invite your network to check in with you. Play around with a few options to find which works best for you.

Regardless of what you choose, it's vital to remember that you never have to do this alone. If you feel stuck, overwhelmed, or unsure of your next steps, don't hesitate to ask for help. Reaching out isn't a weakness; it's a strength that helps you move forward with more confidence and clarity. And if you are worried about burdening others, just think of how you feel when someone asks you for help. You're probably delighted to support your friends and be seen as a trustworthy figure.

Your Don't Dos can also refer to the amount of time you spend on each task. To help allocate an appropriate amount of time to specific tasks, I like to use what I call 'the Olympic Method'. This has saved me and my clients hours of wasted effort. Here's how to use it. Review your tasks, and then determine if each one is a Gold, Silver or Bronze level task.

Gold level tasks require our best attention and need to be done to the highest standard. One example might be giving a TEDx talk, where you'd want every syllable to land perfectly.

Silver level tasks should still be done well, but they don't demand the same level of time and perfection. For example, if you were giving a webinar, you'd want to carefully plan your content so you could deliver real value, but it wouldn't be a big deal if you stumbled over some of your words.

Bronze level tasks just need to get done. This might be a LinkedIn live where you don't need too much preparation, just a clear purpose and a few words on a Post-it to guide you.

If you're like me and most of my clients, you've probably been treating almost every task as a Gold level task. And if that's the case, then applying this method will save you considerable time.

A Time and Energy Audit

Planning how you *want* your days to go is one thing; it can be just as helpful to track how your days *do* go.

List everything you do daily, over a period of two weeks. Review this list and see if there's anything you can delegate, automate or even stop doing entirely. Clearing your schedule of non-essential tasks not only means you'll have the time for your most important tasks, but protects your energy so that you can do them to the best of your ability.

And protecting your energy is what this all boils down to. You are not superhuman – none of us are. You can only deliver your true value if you have the time and energy to be your best self. Carry out frequent energy audits to protect your mental and physical resources and keep on top of your routine.

There are two parts to an energy audit. First, note how you feel at different times of the day. Not all hours are created equal. At certain times we naturally feel more focused; at others we feel more creative, or more social, or more tired, and so on. Once you discover at which times of day you tend to feel a certain way, you can start to map the right activities to those times. You might also note how your energy fluctuates at different times of the month or year. Understanding this can help you plan your projects over the medium to long term. Working with your natural rhythms stops you working against yourself, creating ease, flow and acceptance – and ultimately more impact and growth.

The second part of an energy audit is to do with people, things and activities. For this, on a sheet of paper or in a document, create two columns. At the top of one write a plus sign, and at the top of the other a minus sign. Then list in the first column all the people, things and activities that give you energy, and in the second, those all those that drain you.

Once you have your lists, consider what it is specifically about each person or activity that you find energising or otherwise. For example, you might have written 'Marketing' as something draining; challenge yourself to determine exactly what it is about your marketing that makes you feel this way.

Once you understand these specifics, you can start to address them, either creating a plan to do more of the things in your Energising column, or to minimise the impact of those in the Draining column – or better still, to remove them altogether. You may not be able to make all your changes immediately, but you'll have a plan to work towards.

Your Ideal Schedule

You may have heard of time blocking. It's a classic productivity tool, which requires you to block out time in your diary or schedule to get specific tasks done.

Without question, time blocking is a powerful technique, particularly when you map tasks according to your natural levels of energy and focus as assessed in your energy audit. However, it can take time to get right. Often life gets in the way of our good intentions. We discover that some things take longer than expected, or that we've missed some activities altogether. Suddenly our neat little arrangement of blocks is in ruins.

So when using time blocking, I encourage you to be flexible: create an ideal schedule with the expectation that it will likely prove a challenge. Then, if and when it does, simply adjust it. Over time, you will develop a definitive schedule that you can stick to most of the time.

Remember to include all your non-work tasks too. For a while I didn't understand why I never had the time for everything I set out to achieve. Then I realised that I hadn't included my daily dog walks or added in travel time to certain meetings.

The objective with flexible time blocking is to learn what works for you in practice. If you struggle to get everything onto your schedule, repeat your time audit to see what tasks you can stop or that you can delegate. You may find you need to spread tasks over the month, rather than the week. For example, I might dedicate one week to producing podcasts, the following week to blog content, and so on.

I also like to ask myself: 'How could this be simpler?' I'm a master of overcomplicating things, and this question helps rein me in and encourages me to look for alternative ways to solve a problem or deliver value. It also highlights when I'm wasting time and energy trying to get things 100% perfect. Perfection is a trap. 80% perfect and done today is always better than 100% perfect in theory.

ChatGPT can be a helpful thinking partner when it comes to brainstorming simpler alternatives. And personally, I find a walk in nature – with no distractions (besides my dog) – always helps simplify things in my mind.

When scheduling, employ the Pomodoro technique. The idea is that you work solidly for twenty-five minutes, then take a five-minute break. This helps you to focus more intently and get more done. It also helps you learn how long certain activities *really* take. In practice, I found that twenty-five minutes wasn't quite long enough for some tasks, like writing a blog post or working on this book. So for more creative tasks I work a double Pomodoro: fifty minutes of focus, followed by a ten-minute break where I do some stretches, play with my dog or refill my coffee and dance around the kitchen. Thanks to these regular breaks, I have more energy throughout the day. Try both timings and see what works best for you.

Finally, since we know that few things ever go exactly to plan, I recommend including a buffer in your daily schedule: unallocated time kept in reserve for those inevitable delays, interruptions or complications. If you don't need the buffer, you can choose what to do with your time. Go with whatever feels right in the moment. Do you want to take on an extra task? Spend time connecting with clients, prospects or your network? Or take time out for rest, wellbeing or personal growth? It's always good to have choices.

Success Leaves Clues

'Success leaves clues' is one of those maxims that crops up a lot in the business world. It's generally meant as an encouragement to model successful people in your industry, incorporating what you learn from them into your own way of doing things. It's a great practice. But it should also refer to using *yourself* as a model for success.

Think of a time when you felt proud of a job well done. Then cast your mind back to the environment that led to that success. Where were you? Who were you with? Was there anything that helped you to get started and stay on track – a deadline, supportive colleague, or clear motivation? Remind yourself of all the conditions that you needed to work at your best, and then try and recreate them.

I had this discussion with my Blueprinters a while back, and we discovered that, when they needed to focus, they each favoured different conditions. One felt most focused in a particular café; it had an industrial design and felt slightly unfinished, which helped her feel like she needed to complete her work. For another, it was her home office – but only when it was tidy, with fresh flowers and a scented candle. One found she worked best when taking a boat around Lake Geneva!

When considering your ideal environment, you don't need to think only about focus. When did you feel your most courageous, confident, creative, relaxed, happy? You'll learn a lot about yourself considering such questions, and bit-by-bit you will improve your personal systems, processes and environment, to help you enjoy more of what you want in life.

Creating Boundaries (and Keeping Them)

Once you have your daily tasks and schedule, and you have created your optimum environment, there is just one thing left to do. And that's to stick to your plan! After all, nothing happens if nothing happens.

Creating boundaries will help you stay the course. Here are some steps to help you set and keep your boundaries:

- **Note your boundaries:** Create a simple note for yourself that keeps your goals and plan visible. This could include your working hours, the times when you check your inbox — anything that helps you retain a sense of how your day is best structured. You might not need this once your boundaries become a habit, but it will be helpful in the early days.

- **Communicate your boundaries:** Let those around you know when you will be focused on work, when you can be interrupted, and when you are free. You may need to communicate these boundaries a few times before they are respected consistently!

- **Pause before saying yes:** You have a big heart and love helping people, but you will have more energy and enthusiasm to help others once your own priorities have been met. So before agreeing to any requests, pause and consider *when* you can best help. Instead of a simple 'Yes!' consider something like: 'Yes, I'd love to help you. I can be available after 5pm, does that work for you?'

Also consider if the request matches your skills and value. There may be other tasks you can volunteer for that are a better fit. For example, I was once asked to help organise a local event. However, managing logistics is very much on my 'drains my energy' list. So instead I offered to help market the event. This was an activity the rest of the team had been dreading, so they were delighted to accept.

- **Create an if/then list:** Think ahead to the scenarios that might disrupt your flow and decide how you will respond in advance. For example: '*If* a family member interrupts me, *then* I will gently remind them of my work hours and agree on a time to reconnect.' Or: '*If* a task takes longer than planned, *then* I will pause and assess if it can be scheduled for another time.' This will save you time and energy when planned or unplanned interruptions inevitably arise.

CHAPTER SUMMARY

- Productivity is personal. There is no one-size-fits-all approach.

- The achievement planner grid helps you focus on priorities, manage projects, and avoid overwhelm by breaking tasks into actionable steps.

- Distinguish between tasks and projects. Breaking down big projects into small, manageable actions prevents procrastination and builds momentum.

- Identify your non-negotiables and daily core activities. Prioritise these and create a 'Do Not Do' list to help you stay focused on what matters most.

- Audit your time and energy. Regularly review where your time goes and what energises or drains you. Then align your activities with your natural preferences and rhythms.

- Ask for help when you need it!

- Set clear boundaries, communicate them, plan for interruptions, and use tools like time blocking, buffers, and accountability to support your consistent progress and wellbeing.

Chapter Eleven

Mastering Your Mindset

*You don't have to be loud to make
a difference, but you do need to be
consistently visible to your dream
clients. Your mindset is the key to
doing so comfortably.*

In my first book, *A Shy Girl's Guide to Networking*, I shared how my mindset used to make my life feel so much harder. I dreaded public speaking and networking, and the negative stories I told myself only amplified the fear, making these situations feel almost impossible.

Then a few small mindset shifts changed everything. What once felt terrifying soon became second nature, and before long I was confidently speaking about my network on stages across Europe. Transformation is possible for anyone willing to change the way they think, and this transformation can happen fast.

In that book, I shared my VICTORY Formula, the simple steps I took to turn around my mindset and confidence for good. Since sharing this, I've been truly touched by the messages I've received from readers who used the formula to turn things around in their own lives. Reading their messages, I have gained a deeper appreciation for how powerful mindset can be, and how quickly small changes in our beliefs and thinking can open the door to a new world of possibility.

From coaching, guiding and speaking with thousands of entrepreneurs, I have seen this consistently: one of the biggest challenges to our business growth isn't our skills, budget or the economic climate. It's not our messaging or marketing. It's not even finding the time to do everything we need to. It's our mindset. I could give you the perfect marketing plan, create your perfect sales process, and even add an extra five hours to your day. But if you are held back by negative self-talk, poor self-image or lack of self-belief, none of this will get you results.

The stories we tell ourselves – or more accurately, the *negative* stories we tell ourselves – can hold us back and keep us playing small. And if you want to help people, that is not the space you want to be in.

Mindset is *everything*, and when I finally truly understood this, I became a certified mindset coach so that I had the tools to guide my clients through any doubts or limiting beliefs. Only then could they consistently and successfully market their business with joy, ease and confidence.

Along my own journey of reflection and growth, I reworked the VICTORY Formula into something deeper and more refined. I call it the TRUST Formula. Embrace it, and it might just change your life.

That may sound dramatic, but I really believe it. Just imagine what would happen if you no longer held yourself back – back from that action that will grow your business; back from that practice that will organise your time.

Keep reading, and you won't have to imagine any longer!

The TRUST Formula

Pre-Step: Tune-In

As I've just mentioned, you could complete every step I've outlined in this book – understanding your value, crafting your perfect marketing message suite, creating a winning marketing plan that guides your prospect smoothly and intentionally from 'Hello' to 'Heck yes!' – but without the right mindset, without fully believing in your value, your business won't grow.

Knowing this, why *wouldn't* you take confident action? It all comes back to the stories you tell yourself. The trouble with these stories is recognising that they are stories in the first place. Often you will have been telling them for so long that they feel like the truth.

But once you start to identify which stories are true and which are fiction, you have taken the first step towards freedom – the freedom to take bolder, more confident actions. The next step is to replace these harmful stories with new, empowering truths. But I have to warn you that this process may feel uncomfortable. As Brené Brown says, 'You can't make a difference without first rumbling with vulnerability.'

You don't need to start with all your stories. Start with one, follow the process, feel the difference, and then move on to the next. As you start to expose your false stories, you'll find it easier to identify the next one and so on.

The first step in the TRUST process is to become aware of your negative thoughts, false stories and limiting beliefs. To do this, start paying attention to your thoughts. Pause and tune in any time you notice yourself wavering or procrastinating before taking an action. This is often a sign of a limiting belief. What is the thought that accompanies that hesitation? Notice it, note it down – but, crucially, don't judge it. Instead, simply acknowledge it and add it to your list. It might not be obvious at first, but just keep listening. Sooner or later the thought will surface in your conscious mind.

Maintain a list and then, one thought at a time, follow the TRUTH process outlined below so you can move forward with clarity, renewed enthusiasm and confidence.

T: Test your thoughts
When a negative belief or doubt arises – 'I'm no good at marketing', 'I'm not expert enough', 'No one wants to hear what I have to say' – pause and ask:

- 'Is this true?'

- 'How do I know it's true?'

- 'Is it always true?'

- 'Is there any evidence that this might not be true?'

These questions help you to challenge automatic, unhelpful assumptions and stories. Often, you'll discover that these beliefs are incredibly flawed. For example, maybe you aren't perfect at every aspect of marketing, but there *are* some aspects you excel at. Things are rarely absolute.

R: Release what no longer serves you
Without overthinking your responses, ask yourself:

- 'Who would I be without this thought?'

- 'How would I show up differently?'

- 'What would I do if I didn't believe this limiting idea?'

This starts to open space for a new, more empowering mindset. You may surprise yourself with your answers here, but don't dismiss anything that comes up for you. Instead, sit with your ideas for a while. You might find it helpful to journal on these questions, to bring all the possibilities to the surface.

U: Uncover new possibilities

Now you've glimpsed how things could be different, it's time to explore your new possibilities. Ask yourself:

- 'Could I take that confident action today, even in a small way?'

- 'Could the opposite of my doubt be true?'

The first question gives you the chance to challenge your limiting belief further. If you can take even one small action, it suggests that your original thought isn't true, or at least not entirely true.

The second question helps you see things differently. You can play around with different versions of your question, turning the words around. For example, could you argue that, in fact, you are *good* at marketing? If you start looking around for evidence to support such an argument, you might be surprised by what you find. Which brings us to...

S: Seek supporting truths

Look for evidence that supports your strengths, successes, and potential. This is similar to the exercise in Chapter Eleven, where you were looking for clues in your past successes.

- 'When have I done something similar before?'

- 'What positive feedback have I received?'

- 'What small wins prove that I *can* do this?'

Then, create an empowering truth that reflects your new understanding and feels authentic, supportive and believable. For example: 'I'm good at marketing when I have the time to create content based on a clear strategy' or 'I'm good at marketing when I choose an approach that feels aligned to my personality, skills and vision'.

T: Take action

Many people wait to have confidence before taking action. But the truth is, confidence is what you get *after* taking courageous action – it's the result not the requirement. And even small actions count.

Undertaking any new project or activity takes courage, especially when it's something that you don't feel naturally inclined to do. But if you constantly rely on courage, you will soon end up an exhausted, nervous wreck. The good news is, each time you take courageous action, you build confidence – the belief that you have the capability to do something. And the more confidence you build, the more positive business-building actions you can take, and the less energy and effort it will take to complete them.

Here's a quick example. Recently I *courageously* reached out to three big names in my industry to invite them to join me on my podcast. When all three said yes (and after I'd finished dancing around my living room), I *confidently* reached out to five more big-name guests. That first experience showed me that I could trust my actions, and trust is what turns courage into confidence.

But confidence is also dynamic; it can fade with time. So once you have built it, you want to take steps to maintain it. Ask these questions to help you:

- 'What are the actions you need to take to move your business forward?'

- 'Which of these require courage?'

- 'What is the smallest courageous step you can take?'

- 'When will you take it?'

- 'Once you've succeeded, how will you celebrate?'
- 'Once you've proven to yourself that you are able to take that step, what step will you take next?'

An important part of the process is celebrating each courageous step. This is more than just a nice thing to do for yourself – it's vital to making your progress stick. When you celebrate a win, even in small ways, you signal to your mind that your effort and progress matter. This positive reinforcement makes it easier to keep showing up, even when things get tough or doubts start to loom. It also strengthens your trust in your capabilities, which further builds your confidence.

It's not just a matter of being kind to yourself. The TRUST Formula is holistic: when you break your goals into small milestones, you give yourself more cause to celebrate and acknowledge your ability to make positive progress, and that in turn builds your confidence and momentum faster.

Building Your Mindset through Daily Practice

The TRUST Formula is a powerful way to overturn any negative thoughts and beliefs holding you back. But to build and maintain your success mindset, it can be helpful to incorporate some universally useful habits. Read through the following list, then choose one or two to start with. Practice them daily for a month until they become part of the way you do things, then add in another practice and so on.

1. Practice Daily Gratitude

This is my favourite practice and one I recommend you start with. It's quick and easy, and you can see results relatively quickly too. Here's what to do.

Take a couple of minutes at the end of each working day to jot down at least three things you're grateful for. It may feel weird or difficult at first, but you'll soon find yourself writing long lists of things you've found to appreciate in each day. You can be grateful for big things like a new client or a perfect speaking opportunity; small things like the smile the bus driver gave you, or the joy at opening the dishwasher to find your kids have emptied it; and everything in between. You can even be grateful for past experiences that gave you a certain skill or insight, or for things to come in the future. Over time, your gratitude practice will train your mind to find positives everywhere, which will build your resilience, confidence and joy.

2. Keep a Success Journal

This is another simple but powerful practice that you can start straight away. Keep track of and celebrate your wins, big and small. Alongside each entry, note and show appreciation for how you made each success possible. Over time, this will help you recognise your strengths and build your confidence. Include positive feedback from clients, coaches, friends and colleagues too.

Read through your Success Journal during 'wobble moments', tough days, or to help get in the right mindset before an important meeting or sales conversation. Reminding yourself of your abilities builds the quiet confidence that propels you forward.

3. Embrace the 'Fascinating!' Mindset

I learned this from my last boss before I started my own business, and it has been incredibly useful in preventing me from wallowing in failure, and ensuring that I instead extract the lessons to fuel my growth and future success.

Here's what to do. When things don't go to plan, instead of judging yourself, pause and say, 'Fascinating!' Get curious about what happened, find the lesson, and reflect on how you could apply it in the future. Do this, and you'll enjoy a journey of continual growth.

4. Schedule Learning

Make personal growth a daily habit by setting aside time each day to learn. Even taking ten minutes a day to read a chapter of a book, listen to a podcast, or watch an inspiring video adds up fast. Block time for it in your daily schedule (what is scheduled gets done), along with an extra couple of minutes to reflect on what you've just learned and how you might use that insight in your business or life.

5. Network Regularly

Networking is an important marketing and business growth activity. But it can also help you grow your confidence. When you build genuine relationships, some of those people will open new doors for you, offer fresh perspectives, challenge your doubts, and provide the encouragement, guidance and support you need to dream bigger and achieve more in life and business.

If this isn't something you enjoy or feel you do well today, then my book *A Shy Girl's Guide to Networking* will help you gain the skills and confidence to quickly excel in this area, even if you feel shy today.

6. Prioritise Self-Care

Taking time to look after yourself isn't just about your wellbeing, energy and focus. It's also central to your success. When you prioritise yourself and your needs, putting them to the top of your to do list, you signal to your unconscious mind that you are important and worthy. In turn, this helps you to protect your boundaries, and supports your confidence and continued progress.

Self-care can be about big gestures, like spa days and time away from the business, but it should also be about your positive daily habits, like those you included in your daily achievement planner. Drinking two litres of water each day, going to bed one hour earlier, exercising daily, taking regular breaks, eating healthy meals, including quiet reflection time in your day – these are all self-care. Small actions like these boost your clarity, creativity, and resilience, so you can show up as your best self all day long.

And before you say, 'Yes but...' let me share how my good friend and behavioural psychologist, Lynda Heffernan, describes it: 'Prioritising your own needs is not being selfish, but self-full.'

Create Your SOS Plan

Now you have your TRUST Formula and daily habits, you can start building a more confident, energised, successful you. But even with the best of intentions, life sometimes throws us off course.

Your SOS Plan provides you with a quick and gentle reset whenever you need it. It's a simple list of go-to actions, uplifting reminders, and comforting rituals that help you return to your centre when things feel tough, off balance or overwhelming.

Here are some ideas of things you might like to include in your personal SOS Plan:

- A favourite song that lifts your mood and gets you dancing.

- A quote that inspires, grounds or uplifts you.

- A simple feel-good ritual, like taking a bath or a walk in nature.

- A reminder of your favourite centring practice.

- A way to quickly reassess or reprioritise.

- A brief reminder of your goals and highest vision.

- A grounding mantra or affirmation.

- A pre-recorded pep talk.

- A reminder to review your Success Journal.

- A reminder to contact your accountability buddy.

- A micro-goal checklist, to help you quickly move into action

What you include in your SOS Plan is up to you. You know what best resets your mood and focus. Build your plan over time, keep it somewhere easy to access, and reach for it whenever you need a boost. It's not about fixing anything broken; it's about having support and compassion on hand when you need it most, so you can get back into flow with clarity and confidence.

CHAPTER SUMMARY

- Mindset is the foundation of authentic marketing and steady business growth. Your beliefs and self-talk can either hold you back or propel you forward. Becoming aware of them can help you ensure they do the latter.

- The TRUST Formula (Test, Release, Uncover, Seek, Take Action) provides a practical process for challenging limiting beliefs and building quiet confidence through small, courageous steps.

- Daily practices such as gratitude, success journaling, adopting a 'Fascinating!' mindset, and self-care help sustain a positive, growth-oriented outlook.

- Confidence follows courageous action, not the other way around. Note and celebrate every win, even the smallest ones, to build and reenforce your confidence and create momentum.

- Having a personalised SOS Plan containing uplifting reminders, rituals, and micro-actions will help you quickly reset when facing self-doubt or overwhelm.

- Ultimately, a supportive mindset enables you to show up, serve your dream clients, and enjoy consistent growth, without draining your energy or needing to be loud.

Chapter Twelve

A Recap of Our Journey

You don't have to be the loudest to be successful. The key is to be aligned with your values, so your every action has purpose and meaning.

Success isn't about being the loudest. It's about knowing your value and purpose and aligning with it. It's about sharing your message clearly and consistently. It's about delivering your difference to the right people over the long-term. Whispering your value consistently creates deep resonance, impact and sustainable success.

As you take your True Value out into the world, here are some quick reminders to help you stay true to the Value Whispering Blueprint™.

Your Way Works

There's no single 'right way' to market, sell or grow your business. Likewise, there is no 'ultimate way' to manage yourself, your energy or your focus. Remember your personal blueprint, which is grounded in your strengths, values, vision and purpose, and remind yourself that it is your differences that set you apart and make you so valuable. And remember that you will evolve over time. Trust yourself, take consistent action and keep refining your approach as you grow.

Consistency Over Perfection

Progress, not perfection, is what matters. The real secrets to success are staying consistent, showing up, sharing your value and serving your dream clients according to what you believe works best.

Growth Is a Journey

You are never finished. While you are already an expert at what you do, mastery takes time and it's driven by your vision and passion. Business (and self-leadership) is an ongoing process of learning, adapting and evolving. Enjoy every step you take, show gratitude for your progress (no matter how small), and know that while 'future you' will move mountains, you are already perfectly placed to create a positive impact in the lives of others.

Celebrate Your Difference

Your True Value is unique to you, and this uniqueness is your greatest asset. Embrace the way that *you* create impact.

Cherish Mistakes

Cherish your missteps as much as your wins; each one contains valuable lessons about what it takes for you to succeed. Each one will help you serve your clients deeper, become stronger, stand out with confidence, become more resilient, and create longer-lasting success.

Whisper Your Value

You don't need to shout to be seen. By truly understanding and communicating your value, you'll create a resonance that naturally attracts the right clients and opportunities to you. And every time you whisper your value boldly and authentically, you give others permission to do the same.

I'd like to remind you of the mining for diamonds analogy I shared in the introduction. When you take the time to reveal your diamond within, polish it and proudly share it with the world, you create a kaleidoscope effect that creates positive impacts in unpredictable ways, casting rainbows on any surface it touches.

Every small step you take has the power to transform not only your business, but the lives of the people around you. You may never know the full extent of your impact, but trust that when you base everything you do on your Value Sweet Spot, that impact cannot *not* take place. So, take each step forward with courage, joy and pride.

To help you do that, I have just one thing left to share with you: my Value Whispering Manifesto. You can download a printable version from: www.melittacampbell.com/valuewhisperingbook

The Value Whispering Manifesto

You don't have to be the **loudest**
to have the **biggest impact**.

Your value isn't found in how loud you shout
– it's in **how deeply you resonate**.

The right people – the ones who need
your **unique brilliance** – will
recognise you when you **dare** to show up
with **courage**, **intention** and **heart**.

You are enough.
Your work matters.
Your voice is powerful.

Keep **whispering your value**.
And **watch with pride** as your business and impact **grow**.

Acknowledgments

Looking back over the experiences that have shaped the *Value Whispering* approach has been a real joy. Writing this book has prompted me to remember so many special people and to relive significant moments I hadn't thought about in years.

I always dread the question I'm asked in interviews and on podcasts: "Who has inspired you the most?" The truth is, I take something meaningful from every interaction. When you're open to it, every conversation teaches you something, connects ideas you didn't realise belonged together, and sparks your next step. A wonderful example of this was listening to Brené Brown and Adam Grant discussing her new book on the Dare to Lead podcast. Even in that conversation, they uncovered fresh insights simply by exploring ideas together. I'm looking forward to seeing where the conversations sparked by this book take both me and you.

There are, however, a few people I want to thank specifically.

Firstly, to the lady who threw me out of that interview two decades ago. That single moment set my life and work on an entirely new path. And to all the mentors before and since who helped me recognise my own val-ue and the value in others. I share more of those lessons and turning points in episode 196 of The Art of Value Whispering: "Borrow My Mentors".

Thank you to the coaches who have helped me find clarity and confidence at each stage of my business. In particular, thank you to Matthew Pollard, who helped me discover the term "Value Whispering" in the first place. And thank you to the clients who encouraged me when I was unsure about embracing it fully and who said, with absolute conviction, that it described exactly how our work together felt.

To all the Blueprinters past, present and future – thank you
for trusting me to accompany you as you build businesses that reflect your true value. Your courage, breakthroughs and passion inspire me every day.

To the incredible women in my network, and to the Impossible Society, thank you for walking alongside me. There are far too many of you to name, but I want to give special thanks to Lynda Heffernan and Monica Antohi, who are always my loudest cheerleaders. You help me quiet the familiar voice that asks, "Who am I to do this?" and remind me to think bigger about how I bring Value Whispering into the world.

This book would not exist without the guidance of some remarkable book mentors and coaches, including Alison Jones, Amy Warren and Mindy Gibbins, who each helped me shape the structure and draw the words out of my head and onto the page. Thank you also to my generous pre-readers, whose thoughtful feedback helped me make this book as clear and helpful as possible. And to my publisher, Shaun Russell at Candy Jar Books, and my wonderful editor, William Rees, whose skill, insight and encouragement strengthened this book in every way. I am deeply grateful for our collaboration.

And finally, to you, the reader. Writing a book is one thing, but its true meaning comes alive only when someone like you chooses to explore its ideas and bring them into the world. Thank you for having the courage to uncover your own value, to mine for the diamond within you and to let its light shine in ways only you can.

If this book supports you, I hope you'll pass it on to someone who might need it too, or invite me to share these ideas with your community. Nothing would make me happier than seeing the ripple effect of Value Whispering reach even more people who are ready to make a difference.

Thank you for being part of this journey, and for the light you bring to this world.

About the Author

Melitta Campbell is a business coach, bestselling author and creator of the Value Whispering approach to marketing and communication. Known to many as the Value Whisperer, she has spent three decades helping leaders and entrepreneurs find the clarity, confidence and language to express their true value with ease.

Her career began in the corporate world and later evolved into a consultancy where she supported organisations of all sizes as a communications and leadership expert. Through this blend of internal and consulting work across the private, public and global NGO sectors, Melitta saw firsthand how people flourish when they understand themselves, believe in their unique value and allow that belief to shape not just their words, but how they show up, make decisions and build relationships.

This insight became the foundation of her Value Whispering system: a compassionate, practical framework that helps people uncover the strengths at the heart of their work and translate them into clear, confident communication that feels natural. Through her coaching, workshops, books, TEDx and global speaking engagements, as well as The Art of Value Whispering podcast, Melitta has guided thousands of individuals to market and grow their businesses in a way that honours who they are, not who they think they're supposed to be.

Melitta is driven by a simple belief: when people truly believe in their value, expressing it becomes effortless, and that authenticity creates meaningful ripples in their communities, families and industries. She is especially passionate about empowering more women to step forward with confidence and contribute their brilliance to a world that urgently needs their perspectives. Women's voices have been missing from many of the systems and decisions that have shaped our societies, and Melitta is committed to helping close that gap so our future is more balanced, resilient and human.

Originally from Wales and now based in Switzerland, Melitta lives with her husband, two daughters and Isla, their good-humoured and ever-supportive dog who keeps the whole household smiling.

This book is an invitation to slow down, tune in and discover what makes you remarkable. As you continue your journey, Melitta hopes you'll share these ideas with others and trust that when you consistently whisper your value, you create a legacy that reaches far beyond your work and into the lives of others.

www.melittacampbell.com